Mastering Computer Typing

Mastering Computer Typing

A Painless Course for Beginners and Professionals

Sheryl Lindsell-Roberts

Houghton Mifflin Company
Boston   New York

Library of Congress Cataloging-in-Publication Data

Lindsell-Roberts, Sheryl.
    Mastering computer typing / Sheryl Lindsell-Roberts.
        p.   cm.
    ISBN 0-395-71406-0
    1. Electronic data processing—Keyboarding.   I. Title.
QA76.9.K48L57   1995
652.5—dc20   94-41777
                                                    CIP

Manufactured in the United States of America

DOC 18 17 16

For information about this and other Houghton Mifflin trade and reference books and multimedia products, visit The Bookstore at Houghton Mifflin on the World Wide Web at http://www.hmco.com/trade/.

Acknowledgments

Keyboard drawings by Daniel J. Morin

Book design by Publishers' Design and Production Services, Inc.

Lotus 1-2-3 are registered trademarks of Lotus Development Corporation.

WordPerfect is a registered trademark of Novell, Inc.

Microsoft, MS, and MS-Dos are registered trademarks of Microsoft Corporation.

UNIX is a registered trademark in the United States and other countries and is licensed exclusively through X/Open Company Ltd.

Contents

I *Introduction*

Getting Started

Who Needs to Type?

You do! Whether you're a student, secretary, office administrator, manager, computer programmer, or engineer—whether you use a PC, laptop, or typewriter—typing is an invaluable skill. It's a skill that can open doors and enhance your career opportunities. In this high-tech world of computer-generated communications (fax, electronic mail, word processing, networks, bulletin boards, and much more), anyone who can't type runs the risk of being excluded from many business transactions.

About This Book

This book is designed for self-instruction or classroom instruction. You will be guided through each module, or unit of instruction, in a sequential and logical manner and will join millions of typists who have become proficient through this step-by-step method of learning to type. You will begin your development by typing simple words and will proceed through a wide array of practical applications.

The book is divided into four sections, each with a different purpose.

1. The *Introduction* includes information on hardware and software, computer applications and procedures, and ways to avoid office aches and pains.
2. *Learning to Type* acquaints you with the keyboard through numerous practice exercises.
3. *Practical Applications* presents real-world applications for using a computer, including charts, letters, manuscripts, and computer-related exercises.

4. The *Appendixes* contain a variety of timed typings that you can use as you progress through the book, a glossary of computer terms, and a guide to punctuation.

"Brain Busters" are included in each module. They are not meant to measure your intelligence, clean up the environment, or pay off the national debt. They are intended to give you something to think about while having, I hope, a little fun.

Note   All the exercises in this book are shown in a Courier 12 font (sometimes called Courier 10cpi). If you're using a font other than Courier 12, your output will not match the book line for line. That's OK.

Your Software User Manual

Computer software performs tasks that were once laborious on a typewriter, and each software program will handle these tasks differently. Therefore, please keep the User Manual that came with your software available for reference because you will be asked to use it periodically. Each time you are requested to refer to your User Manual, the words *User Manual* will appear in the margin. You will also be advised which functions you should learn.

Your Objective

Your primary objective should be to touch-type; that is, to type without looking at your fingers. If you turn your head back and forth between the keyboard and the copy, you will not only give yourself a stiff neck but will also slow down, make errors, and lose your place.

Although this book can teach you to type in 24 hours, each person learns at a different pace. Your progress will depend on your past typing experiences and your determination.

Know Your Equipment ──────────────

When you are typing on a typewriter, your input (typing) appears directly on paper. When you are typing on a computer, your input appears on a screen and is transferred to paper (known in the computer arena as *output* or *hard copy*) after the proper command has been given. Get to know your computer. Refer to the instruction manual that accompanies your hardware if you have any questions.

Computer Configuration

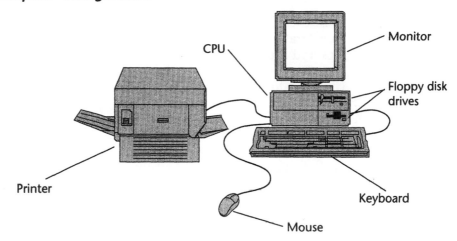

Description of Components

CPU (Central Processing Unit)   The computer's brain that receives the commands from the keyboard. The CPU is the primary storage and processing unit for the information in the computer.

Monitor   A television-like screen on which your text and graphics will be displayed. It is also known as a CRT (cathode-ray tube), display screen, or VDT (video display terminal).

Printer   The peripheral that generates paper copy.

Mouse   A little hand-held device with one or more buttons on top. When you move the mouse on the surface of your desk, you show where the cursor is. Clicking the mouse can also replace some keyboard commands.

Floppy Disk Drives   The slots in the computer where you place your floppy disks.

Keyboard   A standardized "QWERTY" keyboard that will be found on all computers, word processors, and typewriters.

    If you look at the top row of letters, you will notice the QWERTY sequence. All alphabetical keys and numbers will appear in the same place no matter what piece of equipment you are using. Some symbols, punctuation marks, or special keys may differ from one keyboard to another and some enhanced keyboards may include a second set of function keys and other special or duplicate keys, so you should always check the location of the special keys on the keyboard you are using.

#15: TRAUMATIC TALES

1. Wizard of Oz
2. Jack Sprat
3. Jack and the Beanstalk
4. Tom Sawyer
5. Humpty Dumpty
6. Owl and the Pussycat
7. Goldilocks
8. Cinderella
9. Snow White
10. Little Bo Peep

Keyboard

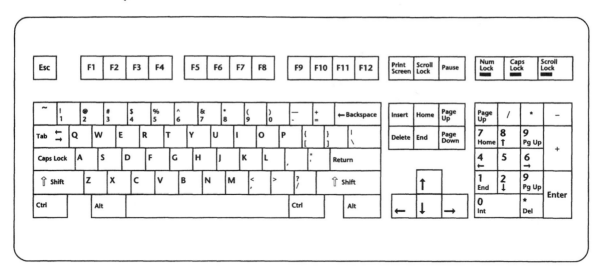

Brain Buster #1:   QWERTY

Think of three 10-letter words that can be typed from the top row keys only.

1. _____

2. _____

3. _____

#12: HYPERBOLES, METAPHORS, AND CLICHÉS

1. raining cats and dogs
2. so hungry I could eat a horse
3. eating us out of house and home
4. as old as Methuselah
5. busy as a one-armed paper hanger; busy as a bee
6. talk one's ears off
7. so mad I could spit nails
8. like a bat out of hell
9. know the place like the back of my hand
10. reads every book published

#13: GOOF-PROOF

1. Remember never **to split an** infinitive.
2. A verb should agree with **its** subject.
3. Proofread carefully to see if words **were** left out **or repeated.**
4. A writer shouldn't shift **his or her** point of view.
5. If any word is **im**proper at the end of a sentence, **it is** a linking verb.
6. Take the bull by the **horns** and never mix metaphors.
7. Always **pick the** correct idiom.
8. Remember, a preposition isn't a word **with which** you should end a sentence.
9. **Avoid clichés.**
10. Avoid trendy **expressions.**

#14: SIMPLY STATED

1. Like father, like son.
2. People in glass houses shouldn't throw stones.
3. Beggars can't be choosers.
4. Don't cry over spilled milk.
5. Beauty is only skin deep.
6. All that glitters is not gold.
7. Honesty is the best policy.
8. United we stand; divided we fall.
9. Don't judge a book by its cover.
10. A bird in the hand is worth two in the bush.

Fonts

Monospacing vs. Proportional Spacing

On a typewriter all the letters are evenly spaced, as if they were in a grid. This is known as monospacing. On a computer you have the option of using letters that are monospaced or proportionally spaced. Proportional spacing means that the width of the character depends on its size. For example, the letter *m* takes up more space than the letter *i*.

```
This is an example of monospacing. All the
letters are evenly spaced.
```

This is an example of proportional spacing. The letters are spaced according to size.

Font Styles

This is an example of serif type called Times Roman, which has little finishing lines on the letters.

This is an example of sans serif type called Helvetica, which has no little finishing lines on the letters.

This is an example of italic.

This is an example of bold.

THIS IS AN EXAMPLE OF SMALL CAPS.

Font Sizes

This is 8 point Times Roman.

This is 10 point Times Roman.

This is 12 point Times Roman.

This is 18 point Times Roman.

This is 24 point Times Roman.

#9: WHO'S AFRAID?

1. claustrophobia
2. agoraphobia
3. aquaphobia
4. xenophobia
5. verbaphobia
6. hematophobia
7. acrophobia
8. nyctophobia
9. gamophobia
10. arachibutyrophobia

#10: RED, WHITE, AND BLUE

1. blackmail
2. talks a blue streak
3. yellow-bellied
4. red-carpet treatment
5. give the green light
6. tickled pink
7. in the limelight
8. brown bag it
9. whitewash
10. wearing rose-colored glasses

#11: SEASCAPES

1. runs a tight ship
2. bailout
3. from stem to stern
4. harbor a grudge
5. hit the deck
6. don't rock the boat
7. all washed up
8. give leeway
9. steer clear of
10. between the devil and the deep blue sea

Justification ————————————————————

On a computer you can select various justifications (or alignments).

Left Justify

Paragraphs align at the left. This is the primary style when you are using a typewriter, because at the end of a line you press the carriage return and advance to the next line. It is also very popular for computers.

Full Justify or Justify

Many of us are used to seeing this type of justification in books and publications. When you use this type of justification, be careful you do not create unusual spacing between words that can cause rivers (streaks of white space) that flow down the page.

Center Justify

Everything is centered. If you are using a typewriter, this must be done manually. This is a popular style for headings, invitations, announcements, etc.

Right Justify

All your text appears at the right. This is generally reserved for special circumstances such as invitations, announcements, etc.

#6: LETTER PERFECT

1. letters of the alphabet
2. Arabian Nights
3. signs of the zodiac
4. planets in the solar system
5. keys on a piano
6. stripes on the American flag
7. degrees at which water freezes
8. degrees in a right angle
9. sides on a stop sign
10. quarts in gallon

#7: BEASTASAURUS REX

1. night owls
2. fighting like cats and dogs
3. play possum
4. pigheaded
5. no spring chicken
6. talk turkey
7. guinea pig
8. straw that broke the camel's back
9. eats like a pig
10. goose that laid the golden egg

#8: FOODAHOLIC

1. nuts; bananas
2. in a jam; in a pickle
3. lemon
4. butter up
5. long drink of water
6. bowl of cherries
7. slow as molasses
8. piece of cake; easy as pie
9. that's the way the cookie crumbles
10. carrot-top

Borders and Rules _____

There are many features available on a computer that are not available on a typewriter. Here are some examples of what you can create on a computer.

Single-Border Box

> This is an example of a single-border box.

Double-Border Box

> This is an example of a double-border box.

Shadow Box

> This is an example of an unshaded shadow box.

Shaded Shadow Box

> This is an example of a shaded shadow box.

Assorted Rules

Typing Tidbits _____

Computers allow much more versatility than typewriters, so there are many new ways of displaying information.

Spacing   As a general rule, space once after a punctuation mark, including the period at the end of a sentence.

Dash   When you type a dash, use the special dash symbol (—), not two hyphens.

Apendix D
BRAIN BUSTER ANSWERS

#1: QWERTY

1. typewriter
2. proprietor
3. perpetuity

#2: 28-LETTER WORD

antidisestablishmentarianism

#3: THREE CONSECUTIVE DOUBLE LETTERS

bookkeeping *or* bookkeeper

#4: CONSECUTIVE VOWELS

1. seeing
2. sequoia
3. queueing

#5: OXYMORONS

1. live
2. opposition
3. deviation
4. justice
5. teacher
6. silverware
7. order
8. ugly
9. War
10. news

Emphasis	Underscoring is passé. With typewriters, the underscore is the only way to emphasize something. With computers, *italics*, **bold**, or SMALL CAPS are more appropriate.
Quotes	Use quotation marks (" ") rather than the inch symbol (") for quoted material.
Accent and Diacritical Marks	Accent and diacritical marks are available with many software packages. Use them when you can. For example:

niño   Übermensch
à coup sûr   garçon

Special Symbols There are also special symbols available. Here are just a few.

© copyright   π   pi
® registered trademark   ™   trademark

Avoiding Aches, Pain, and Fatigue ———————————

Office aches, pain, and fatigue . . . Why suffer? A simple modification of your workspace and habits, and a little exercise done at your desk, can go a long way in preventing pain in the neck, shoulders, and back; headaches; eye strain; fatigue; carpal tunnel syndrome (CTS) or tendinitis; and a host of other pains and injuries associated with sedentary occupations.

Ergonomics

Ergonomics is a term that combines the Greek word *ergon,* meaning "work," and the English word *(eco)nomics,* which ultimately goes back to a Greek word that means "one who manages a household." Simply stated, it is "the study and management of the relationship between the worker and the environment." Ergonomics addresses the physical, physiological, and psychological requirements of each of us. In this section, we discuss the physical requirements.

Seating Because you'll spend most of your time seated, one of the most important components is your chair. Look for a chair that has a sturdy base with four or five legs set on free-wheeling casters. It should also have armrests to help relieve the pressure on the wrist.

QUOTATION MARKS

Note

Commas and periods always go inside quotation marks. Colons and semico-lons always go outside quotation marks. Question marks and exclamation points go inside quotation marks when they apply to the quoted material only. They go outside when they apply to the entire sentence. For example:

```
She asked, "Did you finish the English course?"
```

```
Why did you call that task "impossible"?
```

- To surround something or someone being directly quoted (exact words):

```
"I like your idea," Mr. James commented.
```

- To enclose titles of articles, short poems, lectures or topics, paintings, short stories, or chapters:

```
In THE SECRETARY'S QUICK REFERENCE HANDBOOK there's
a chapter entitled "Desktop Publishing."
```

- To set off words or phrases introduced by an expression such as *the word, known as, called,* etc.

```
The check was marked "canceled."
```

- To set off words that are used in an unconventional manner:

```
He is "hot stuff."
```

UNDERSCORE

Note

Instead of the underscore, use *italics*, ALL CAPS, or SMALL CAPS to set off titles of books, magazines, movies, pamphlets, brochures, long poems, plays, or other literary works:

```
I read The New York Times every Sunday.
```

```
I read THE NEW YORK TIMES every Sunday.
```

Courtesy of Grahl Industries, Clearwater, MI

The seat pan and cushion should accommodate your hips and buttocks without being too snug. The pan should be adjustable to tilt slightly forward for writing and slightly backward for keyboarding. If the seat pan isn't adjustable, look for a wedge-shaped cushion that can be positioned one way for writing and another for keyboarding. Lumbar cushions are available in a variety of shapes and sizes for proper body alignment.

Look for a chair that can be raised and lowered to accommodate your height so that your feet rest comfortably on the floor. Your calves should be perpendicular to the floor and your knees slightly higher than your hips to avoid excessive curvature of the lower back. If your feet don't rest comfortably on the floor, a slanted footrest can help support them.

Make sure that all mechanical adjustments on your chair can be made while you are seated.

Note   Even the best-designed chair won't make up for bad posture. Bad posture is the root of many physical problems. Your spine consists of interconnected bones, known as vertebrae. They form three major curves in your neck, back, and lower back. If these curves become flattened or exaggerated due to poor posture, your spine will be out of whack and you can experience pain. So, sit upright and don't slouch. Your back should be straight to support the upper part of your body.

- To set off references to charts, pages, diagrams, etc.:

  `The section on dinosaurs (pages 145—149) should be . . .`

- To enclose numerals or letters that precede items in a series:

  `I can be there on (1) Monday, June 1; (2) Tuesday, June 2; or (3) . . .`

BRACKETS

- To include information added to something or someone being quoted:

  `He said, "The length of the trial [from May 1 through June 15] caused . . . "`

- To enclose parenthetical information within parentheses:

  `Your order (which included a dozen red pens [that are not available] and five dozen blue pens) will be . . .`

QUESTION MARKS

- At the end of a direct question:

  `May we expect you by noon tomorrow?`

- After each question in a series of short questions that relate to the same subject and verb:

  `Can you be there on Monday, June 1? Or on Tuesday, June 2?`

- When a sentence begins as a statement and ends as a question:

  `The store made the delivery on September 16, didn't they?`

- To express uncertainty about a stated fact:

  `On September 16 (?) the store made the delivery.`

Work Surface The work surface for the average person—whatever *average* really means—should be between 26 and 29 inches from the floor. You'll be most comfortable when the work surface is slightly above elbow height. This allows you to rest your arms on the surface without leaning too far forward. An adjustable shelf for the keyboard will help lessen the strain on your forearms and wrists.

Monitor Headaches and eyestrain can result from being too close or too far from the monitor. The monitor should be between 18 and 28 inches away from you, and the top of the screen should be even with your forehead.

Keyboard The proper height and position of the keyboard are essential to avoiding wrist problems, such as CTS and tendinitis. Your best defense is a natural, relaxed position. Your arms should hang comfortably at your sides so that your shoulders aren't hunched. And your forearms should be at 90 degree angles to your arms. You don't want to reach up or down to the keyboard. To take the weight off your shoulders and back, rest your forearms on the armrests of your chair. Keep your fingers curved and placed as close to the keys as possible.

There are devices on the market that are designed to protect against repetitive stress injuries. One of these devices is a wrist rest, which can be positioned below the keyboard. There is also a rest available for the mouse.

Courtesy of Computer Expressions, Inc., Philadelphia, PA

Avoiding Aches, Pain, and Fatigue

- Before expressions such as for example, that is, namely, etc.:

  That's available in two colors; namely, blue and green.

COLONS

- After a formal introduction that includes or implies *the following*:

  We expect to open new offices in each of these locations: New Bedford, . . .

- To introduce a long direct quotation:

  Senator Longwinded said: " . . .

- After a statement that introduces an explanation or example:

  My recommendation is: Don't delay.

DASHES

- To set off a parenthetical expression you want to emphasize:

  The movie—in case you're interested—will be at the . . .

- Before a word that sums up a preceding series:

  Bob, Beth, Donna, and Jim—these are my friends from photography class.

- To indicate a summarizing thought or an afterthought:

  I know that wasn't an easy decision—even for you.

- Before the name of an author or word that follows a direct quote:

  "You can turn painful situations around through laughter. If you can find humor in something, you can survive it."

  —Bill Cosby

PARENTHESES

- To set off a parenthetical expression you want to deemphasize:

  The move (in case you're interested) will be at the . . .

Lighting	Lighting experts have found that indirect, ceiling-mounted, or ambient lighting, in combination with a desk lamp, works best to eliminate problems associated with lighting. If you find that glare and brightness are a problem, purchase an antiglare screen.
Source Documents	Source documents—or this book—should be parallel with the monitor. The viewing distance should be between 24 and 36 inches. Keep your head erect and your eyes on the copy.

Exercises

If you sit for long periods of time, you'll force your muscles into a fixed position, causing fatigue and stiffness. Walking and stretching periodically can help relax the muscles. Try to get away from your desk for at least three minutes every hour. Additionally, simple exercises at your desk can help eliminate fatigue.

Breathing	With your eyes opened or closed, concentrate on breathing. Take five to ten long and deep breaths, inhaling through your nose and exhaling through your mouth.
Eyes	At least once every hour look away from the monitor and focus on an object 15 to 20 feet away. A wonderful exercise for eye relaxation is to rub your hands together briskly until your palms feel warm. Make shallow cups and gently place your palms over your eyes. Without pressing on your eyes, make sure no light enters. Hold your palms over your eyes for at least 30 seconds. For a little variety while your eyes are covered, roll both eyes to the left and back to the middle. Do this five times, then do the same exercise rolling both eyes to the right.
Hands and Wrists	Every 15 to 30 minutes stretch your arms out to your side and over your head. Massage your hands and wrists to improve circulation. Don't forget to massage the spaces between your fingers and the areas around your nails. Flex your fingers and do wrist stretches frequently.
Neck	While breathing deeply, tilt your head toward your left shoulder, then toward your right shoulder. Then, with your head in a forward position, drop your chin to your chest and raise it slightly back. As a variation, keep your head upright. Look over your left shoulder several times, then over your right shoulder several times.

- To set off abbreviations, titles, and degrees that follow a name:

  `Max Lorenz, CPA, will be our guest speaker.`

- To set off contrasting expressions:

  `I'll be on vacation in March, not April.`

- To divide a sentence that starts as a statement and ends as a question:

  `You'll call her, won't you?`

- To separate items in reference works:

  `The answer is in Volume II, Chapter 3, line 12.`

- To separate words that are used for emphasis:

  `You've told me that many, many times before.`

- To separate adjectives in a series if the word *and* has been omitted:

  `She is a very intelligent, thoughtful person.`

- To separate figures that aren't related:

  `In 1994, 250 employees were . . .`

- To clarify a sentence that would otherwise be confusing:

  `Only two weeks before, I had lunch with him.`

SEMICOLONS

- To separate independent clauses in a compound sentence when no conjunction is used:

  `Pete will arrive at ten; George will arrive at eight.`

- To separate independent clauses joined by a conjunction, when two or more commas are used in the sentence:

  `I like green, blue, and red; but she likes . . .`

- Between coordinate clauses of a compound sentence that are joined by a parenthetical word or phrase:

  `We will meet again tomorrow; therefore, the project will continue.`

- To separate items in a series when the items themselves contain commas:

  `I can be there on Monday, June 1; Tuesday, June 2; or Thursday, June 4.`

Back and Arms	Hold your right elbow with your left hand. Gently push the elbow toward your left shoulder. Hold the stretch for five seconds. Repeat this exercise with the left elbow.
	Interlace your fingers and lift your arms over your head, keeping your elbows straight. Press them as far back as you can without causing discomfort.
Note	All these exercises are intended for people who are in reasonably good health. If you experience any pain or discomfort while doing them, stop immediately and consult your doctor.

Appendix C
PUNCTUATION POTPOURRI _____

COMMAS

- Between items in an address or date:

  `On Monday, April 8, 19XX, he . . .`

- To set off an expression that explains the preceding word, name, or phrase:

  `Canal Avenue, our town's main street, will be . . .`

- Before a conjunction with two independent clauses:

  `Pete will arrive at ten, and George will arrive at eight.`

- To set off words that directly address the person to whom you are speaking by name, title, or relationship:

  `Mr. Jones, please tell me . . .`

- After an introductory clause that is followed by what could be a complete sentence:

  `Unless you call, I will assume you will be here.`

- To set off an independent introductory expression that serves as an interjection:

  `Yes, I think so.`

- To set off an expression that if omitted would not change or destroy the meaning of the sentence:

  `My brother, who is wearing a brown suit, is a lawyer.`

- To surround a parenthetical expression of a word, phrase, or clause that interrupts the natural flow of the sentence:

  `We will, therefore, continue with the project.`

- To identify a person who is being directly quoted:

  `"I will be there tomorrow," she indicated.`

- To separate items in a series of three or more items:

  `Bob enjoys ice cream, candy, and potato chips.`

Learning to Type

Module 1
*HOME ROW KEYS*_____

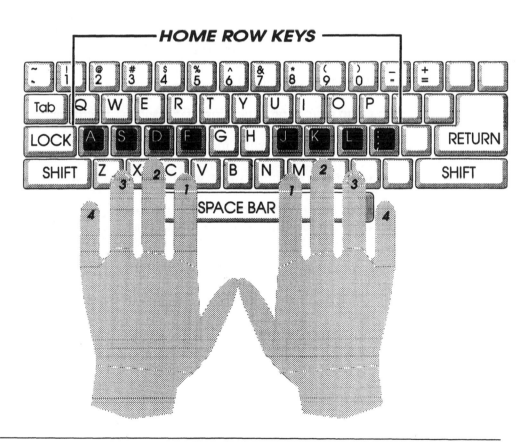

RAM   [*Random-Access Memory*] Information the computer uses to run a program. RAM is temporary memory that is erased when the computer is turned off.

ROM   [*Read-Only Memory*] Information the computer uses to run the systems. ROM is permanent memory that is not erased when the computer is turned off.

sans serif   A typeface without serifs.

> This is an example of sans serif type.

serif   A fine line that finishes the main strokes of a character.

> This is an example of serif type.

software   The programs and routines needed to give a computer instructions.

toggle   To shift, by means of a *toggle switch,* from one operation to another.

UNIX   A PC operating system developed at Bell Laboratories.

uppercase   Letters that are capitalized.

variable   Subject to change or something that is subject to change.

VDT   [*V*ideo *D*isplay *T*erminal] A monitor.

white space A planned area of empty space, giving a document an open and airy look.

WYSIWYG   [*W*hat *Y*ou *S*ee *I*s *W*hat *Y*ou *G*et] A system or program that displays on a screen exactly what you will see on the printed page.

DON'T TURN YOUR COMPUTER ON YET.

HOME ROW

The home row represents the keys on which your fingers will initially be placed and the row to which they will always return.

Left [A][S][D][F]   The keys for your left hand are [A] [S] [D] [F].

Right [J][K][L][;]   The keys for your right hand are [J] [K] [L] [;].

[Space Bar]
[Enter]

Before you start to type, familiarize yourself with two additional keys: [Space Bar] and [Enter]. Find them on your computer.

Finger Positions   Place your fingers on the home row. Your fingers should be slightly curved and as close to the keys as possible.

Now, with a quick stroke, strike the [Space Bar] several times with your left thumb and then several times with your right thumb. Zip your right pinkie to the [Enter] key.

TURN YOUR COMPUTER ON.

Place your fingers on the appropriate keys on the home row and repeat the above exercise until the movement feels comfortable.

Remember:

- Strike [Enter] at the end of each line.
- Keep your eyes on the copy, not on your fingers.

Note   If you're using a font that is proportionally spaced, your letters won't line up at the right margin. That's OK.

Type   SAY EACH LETTER AS YOU STRIKE IT

LAN	[*Local Area Network*] A system in which electronic equipment is connected to form a network within a limited area, such as a building or group of buildings.
landscape	Horizontal page orientation.
leading	[pronounced LED-ing] The amount of vertical space between the tops of the uppercase letters in two successive lines of text.
lowercase	Letters that are not capitalized.
memory	The capacity of a computer to store data and programs. *See also* RAM and ROM.
menu	A list of available options or commands displayed on a monitor.
modem	[*Modulator* + *Dem*odulator] A device that converts data from one form into another, as from digital to analog and vice versa, so that it can be transmitted between a computer and a telephone.
monospacing	Spacing in which each character takes up the same amount of space.
off-line	Not connected to or dependent on a computer or computer network.
on-line	Connected to, dependent on, or accessible by means of a computer or computer network.
output	Data produced by a computer.
peripheral	A piece of equipment, such as a monitor, printer, or modem, that is added to a computer to give it additional functionality.
pica	A unit of type that equals 12 points or 1/6 inch.
pixel	The smallest image-forming unit on a monitor.
point	A unit of measure used to specify type sizes.
program	A sequence of instructions for a computer.
proportional spacing	Spacing in which each character takes up a different amount of space, depending on it size. For example, the character *i* takes up less space than the character *w*.

LEFT HAND ONLY

[A][S][D][F]

```
a aa aaa a aa aaa a aa aaa a aa aaa a aa aaa
a aa aaa a aa aaa a aa aaa a aa aaa a aa aaa

s ss sss s ss sss s ss sss s ss sss s ss sss
s ss sss s ss sss s ss sss s ss sss s ss sss

a aa aaa s ss sss a aa aaa s ss sss a aa aaa
s ss sss a aa aaa s ss sss a aa aaa s ss sss

d dd ddd d dd ddd d dd ddd d dd ddd d dd ddd
d dd ddd d dd ddd d dd ddd d dd ddd d dd ddd

f ff fff f ff fff f ff fff f ff fff f ff fff
f ff fff f ff fff f ff fff f ff fff f ff fff

d dd ddd f ff fff d dd ddd f ff fff d dd ddd
f ff fff d dd ddd f ff fff d dd ddd f ff fff

aa ss dd ff aa ss dd ff aa ss dd ff aa ss dd
aa ss dd ff aa ss dd ff aa ss dd ff aa ss dd

fff aaa sss ddd fff aaa sss ddd fff asdf adf
fff aaa sss ddd fff aaa sss ddd fff asdf adf

asdf asdf asdf asdf asdf asdf asdf asdf
asdf asdf asdf asdf asdf asdf asdf asdf
```

Words

```
a as add adds fad sad a ass add fad fads sad
```

Remember:

- Strike [Enter] at the end of each line.
- Keep your eyes on the copy, not on your fingers.

DOS   [*Disk Operating System*] Software that directs the operations of a computer. Without an operating system, your computer would not know what to do.

downtime   A temporary period during which a computer is not operational.

edit   To revise text.

field   An area in a document for related information, such as names, addresses, or cities. For example:

NAME [   ]

floppy disk Another name for a disk.

font   An assortment of characters for one size and typeface. A font normally includes lightface and **boldface** and roman and *italic* characters and may often include small capitals.

format   The size, style, typeface, page size, margins, and printing requirements of a printed document.

hard copy Computer-generated material that is printed on paper.

hardware   Computer equipment and peripherals.

input   Information that is entered into a system.

interface The interaction, connection, or communication between two or more systems or devices.

justification The alignment of horizontal lines.

- left justify—text aligns at the left margin.
- right justify—text aligns at the right margin.
- center justify—text is centered.
- full justify—text aligns at left and right margins.

kerning   The adjustment of horizontal spaces between letters to make them aesthetically pleasing.

kilobyte (k or K) 1,024 bytes of information or storage space.

RIGHT HAND ONLY

[J][K][L][;]

```
j jj jjj j jj jjj j jj jjj j jj jjj j jj jjj
j jj jjj j jj jjj j jj jjj j jj jjj j jj jjj

k kk kkk k kk kkk k kk kkk k kk kkk k kk kkk
k kk kkk k kk kkk k kk kkk k kk kkk k kk kkk

j jj jjj k kk kkk j jj jjj k kk kkk j jj jjj
k kk kkk j jj jjj k kk kkk j jj jjj k kk kkk

l ll lll l ll lll l ll lll l ll lll l ll lll
l ll lll l ll lll l ll lll l ll lll l ll lll

; ;; ;;; ; ;; ;;; ; ;; ;;; ; ;; ;;; ; ;; ;;;
; ;; ;;; ; ;; ;;; ; ;; ;;; ; ;; ;;; ; ;; ;;;

l ll lll ; ;; ;;; l ll lll ; ;; ;;; l ll lll
; ;; ;;; l ll lll ; ;; ;;; l ll lll ; ;; ;;;

jj kk ll ;; jj kk ll ;; jj kk ll ;; jj kk ll
;; jj kk ll ;; jj kk ll ;; jkl; jkl; jkl; kk
jkl; jkl; jkl; jkl; jkl; jkl; jkl; jk;l kl;k
```

BOTH HANDS

```
a j s k d l f; aa jj ss; kk dd ll ff ;; aa s
a j s k d l f; aa jj ss; kk dd ll ff ;; aa s

a j s k d l f ; aa jj ss kk dd ll ff ;; asjk
a j s k d l f ; aa jj ss kk dd ll ff ;; asjk

; f l d k s j a ;; ff ll dd kk ss jj aa ;; f
; f l d k s j a ;; ff ll dd kk ss jj aa ;; f
```

Appendix B
GLOSSARY

alphanumeric	Consisting of both alphabetical and numeric characters.
ASCII	[*American Standard Code for Information Interchange*] A standard format for representing characters. A text file is in ASCII format.
batch	A collection of similar data that can be produced in a single operation.
bit	[*Binary Digit*] The smallest unit of information in a computer.
byte	A sequence of bits, usually shorter than a word. A byte generally represents eight bits.
character	A letter, number, symbol, space, or punctuation mark.
command	An instruction to the computer to perform a certain function.
cps or *CPS*	[*Characters per Second*] The speed at which characters are generated.
CPU	[*Central Processing Unit*] The brains of the computer.
crash	A sudden failure of a computer program or system.
CRT	[*Cathode-Ray Tube*] A monitor. Also called a *video display terminal* or *VDT*.
cursor	The movable indicator on a computer screen. It is usually an arrow, static I, blinking rectangle, or dash that indicates the place where your next character will appear.
database	A collection of files of information arranged for speed and ease of retrieval.
debug	To locate and remove errors from a computer program.
delete	To remove a character, word, line, paragraph, page, document, file, directory, etc.
disk or *diskette*	A thin, flat circular plate coated with a magnetic substance. It is used for recording and storing data.

Words   a as add ask asks a as add; ask asks sad dad
dads fad fads lad lads; flask lass ask; asks
dad dads; salad salads sad dad dads lad lads
fad fads flask lad;; flask lass ask asks dad
dads; salad salads sad dad dads lad lads fad

LEFT HAND [G]

[F] → [G]   Zip [F] finger to [G]

g gg ggg f ff fff g gg ggg f ff fff g gg ggg
g gg ggg f ff fff g gg ggg f ff fff g gg ggg

a ss ddd f gg aaa s dd fff g aa sss d ff ggg
a ss ddd f gg aaa s dd fff g aa sss d ff ggg

RIGHT HAND [H]

[J] ← [H]   Zip [J] finger to [H]

j jj jjj h hh hhh j jj jjj h hh hhh j jj jjj
j jj jjj h hh hhh j jj jjj h hh hhh j jj jjj

j kk lll ; hh jjj k ll ;;; h jj kkk l ;; hhh
j jj jjj h hh hhh j jj jjj h hh hhh j jj jjj

Words   all fall falls hall halls; glad ash dash ask
as ask gash hash; glass flask lash; slash as
lads glass sash all fall falls hall; halls;;
glad ash dash gash hash glass flask lash all
slash lads glass sash;; fall shall; gash lag

fall hall gash dash lash sash lads; shall had
ash flash; ask flask dash all fall hall; lash
hash dash; asks; flasks halls; falls; has jag
ash flash; ask flask dash all fall hall; lash
all hall gash dash lash sash lads; shall jags

If you are thinking of using your computer to   10
start up a home-based business, here are some tips   20
to keep in mind: Set aside a separate room in your   30
home where you can work; make use of the telephone   40
directory instead of driving in the car; keep your   50
frequently used essentials handy; establish ground   60
rules to keep distractions to a minimum; keep reg-   70
ular hours; establish a routine; establish a back-   80
up system; use a single calendar; break the day up   90
into segments; keep good records; and do not forgo   100
vacations.   102

1   2   3   4   5   6   7   8   9   10

Also, know your market; seek out free public-   10
ity; go after quality clients; prepare a marketing   20
schedule; charge what you are worth; make the most   30
of your billable time; make networking a priority;   40
learn from your mistakes; recognize growing pains;   50
be nice to people; and learn financial management.   60

1   2   3   4   5   6   7   8   9   10

Brain Buster #2:   28-Letter Word

What's a 28-letter word that means "a doctrine against the dissolution of the establish-ment"?

— —

Often, the terms keyboarding and typewriting 10
are used interchangeably. Both are operations that 20
involve data being entered on a keyboard. There is 30
a slight difference. When you are typewriting on a 40
typewriter, your input appears right on the paper. 50
When you are keyboarding on a computer, your input 60
appears on the screen. You have the opportunity to 70
edit and make any changes without ever using those 80
old-fashioned pencil erasers or carbon paper. When 90
you are ready to print a paper copy, you only need 100
to give the computer the command. In a few moments 110
you will have a paper copy of the data you expect. 120

1   2   3   4   5   6   7   8   9   10

The world is full of color. Color adds much impact 10
to anything we see and do. Color can create a mood 20
or help in separating the ripe from the unripe. It 30
has impact on us in a number of ways. For example, 40
red can invoke feelings of danger or excitement or 50
tell us to stop. White is used to represent clean, 60
pure, and honest feelings. Black is used to invoke 70
feelings of heaviness, death, or seriousness. Pink 80
shouts of youth, femininity, and warmth. And green 90
indicates growth, comfort, positiveness, and tells 100
us to go. Color has a lot of meaning to all of us. 110
It's being used in many psychological experiments. 120

1   2   3   4   5   6   7   8   9   10

Module 2
TOP ROW KEYS _____

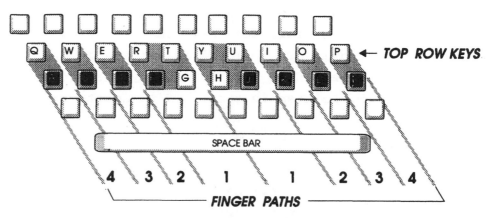

Note: Keys are spaced apart to depict finger paths

You will be moving your fingers off the home row, but they should always return to the original keys on the home row.

[T]

    [T]

   ↗

[F]

Zip [F] finger to [T]

```
f ff fff t tt ttt f ff fff t tt ttt f ff fff
f ff fff t tt ttt f ff fff t tt ttt f ff fff

fftt ftft fftt ftft ff tt ftt fff tt f r trt
fftt ftft fftt ftft ff tt ftt fff tt f r trt
```

WORDS

```
that lath task tall tads dash had tall hall;
fat; flask flat fast; sash tads lads; sat as
halls halts fast asks; dash that shalt shall
fast last all; gash stall lath had tall; all
```

You can use abbreviations for many purposes. There   10
is one basic rule, however: "If in doubt, write it   20
out." Generally, abbreviate academic degrees, such   30
as B.A., M.A., Ph.D., or professional titles, such   40
as R.N., Esq., Rev. Abbreviate the common names of   50
companies, organizations, and government agencies,   60
such as AT&T, MCI, IBM, YMCA, YWCA, FAA, HEW, EPA.   70
Acronyms are formed from letters in long titles or   80
phrases. Some familiar acronyms are OPEC, NOW, and   90
ZIP. Do keep in mind: "If in doubt, write it out."   100

1   2   3   4   5   6   7   8   9   10

Telecommunications is a link between the worlds of   10
word processing and data processing and the audio-   20
visual industry. Telecommunications transmits both   30
oral and written communication from one machine to   40
another in a different location. Cables interfaced   50
with computers allow you to patronize your depart-   60
ment store, query your local library, or ascertain   70
information on your bank accounts. Now, conference   80
calls are used to allow people in remote locations   90
to conduct business meetings without being face to   100
face. Telecommunications curtails time and travel!   110

1   2   3   4   5   6   7   8   9   10

[R]
[R]

↖

[F]

Zip [F] finger to [R]

f ff fff r rr rrr f ff fff r rr rrr f ff fff
f ff fff r rr rrr f ff fff r rr rrr f ff fff

fftt fftt ffrr ffrr ff tt ftt frr tt trtf fr
ttrr ftft fftr ftrr ff rr ftt fff rt rtfr tf

WORDS

hath lath shalt fall rash fast last lash ask
fall falls; asks tall trash grass sash; hats
flask hall halt gash grass lass rash ash; as
rash shalt fall fast; last ask rats rash rag

[E]
[E]

↖

[D]

Zip [D] finger to [E]

d dd ddd e ee eee d dd ddd e ee eee d dd ddd
d dd ddd e ee eee d dd ddd e ee eee d dd ddd

ddee ddee deed eede eded edft edrt reft deft
eede ddde ertf gfrt getd ttfr tred grdt fret

WORDS

ate rag had fat eel eels feel heel slat gall
had sat had fat eels eel heel feel gall slat
tree fled sled held tasks last ask sale tall

glad fled sled held; task last ask sale tall
data date late; talk lath let fatal atlas as
sealed false feeds faded; tested raffle eggs

[U]
[U]

↖

[J]

Zip [J] finger to [U]

j jj jjj u uu uuu j jj jjj u uu uuu j jj j
j jj jjj u uu uuu j jj jjj u uu uuu u uu u

ju jjuu jjuujjuu ju jjuu jjuuj juu uju
ju jjuu jjuujjuu ju jjuu jjuuj juu uju

jjuu jjuu juju juju uujj ujuj jjuu juju juj
jjuu jjuu juju juju uujj ujuj jjuu juju juj

USE CLEAR AND SIMPLE LANGUAGE

When writing, always be sure the language you pick   16
is clear as well as simple. Mark Twain once wrote,   26
"I notice you use plain and simple language, brief   36
sentences. That is the way to write English." That   46
is true whatever you write. Correct word choice is   56
essential to understanding. Why use "utilize" when   66
you mean "use"? Why use "terminate" when you could   76
use "end"? And why use "numerous" when "many" will   86
say it clearly? That IS the way to write English!!   96

1   2   3   4   5   6   7   8   9   10

      The following words are commonly misspelled.   10
How many of them you can type correctly? eligible,   20
appropriate, embarrass, oblige, paid, maintenance,   30
truly, similar, separate, exhaust, minimum, a lot,   40
questionnaire, reference, perseverance, Wednesday,   50
endorsement, knowledge, unanimous, until, foreign,   60
February, forty, unnecessary, sympathy, interpret,   70
extraordinary, feasible, library, dissatisfactory,   80
disbursement, bookkeeping, beneficial, convenient,   90
abbreviation, cannot, bankrupt, its, and surprise.   100

1   2   3   4   5   6   7   8   9   10

WORDS

us lug hug dug sue due just adjust rust after
rested stalk feud feuds feudal fuel fuels has
after as used useful duffle fuss fuse refuses

refused suede auks ukulele restful true user
just adjust; rust gust; hurt hurl; furl dash
shut huts ruts glut ruffle raffle hassle use

[I]
[I]

Zip [K] finger to [I]

[K]

j jj jj i ii ii j jj jj i ii ii ji ji ji
j jj jj i ii ii j jj jj i ii ii ji ji ji

jjii jjii iijj jiji jiji ijij jiii jjjij
jii jjii iijj jiji jiji ijij jiii jjjiji

WORDS

just sits west feast least listed used its
listless tilted asked whisk; whisked; wish
wished washer aid laid said lust list last

waist rut aide aides rust rested listed it
rest; fist fish; gist this that risk; kite
skies skit huts rested tried fried hied it

Let's Shift

[Shift]

There is a [Shift] key on each side of your keyboard. [Shift] keys are used to capitalize letters or type the symbols or characters on the top of the keys on which more than one character is shown.

[Caps Lock]

Locate the [Caps Lock] key on your keyboard. This is used when you want to capitalize a series of letters and do not want to hold down the [Shift].

Left [Shift]

Press the left [Shift] quickly and firmly with your left pinkie while simultaneously pressing any letter with your right hand.

Right [Shift]

Press the right [Shift] in the same manner with your right pinkie and simultaneously press any letter with your left hand.

Commas are used to set off the individual elements   10
of an address except for ZIP codes. As an example,   20
you would write Mr. and Mrs. Arthur Bainless, 2305   30
Main Street, Monsey, NY 10952. If a preposition is   40
used between the elements, you would not place the   50
comma between the elements. As an example, Mr. Jon   60
Doe of One Madison Avenue in Washington, DC 20233.   70

1   2   3   4   5   6   7   8   9   10

What is the most efficient means of communication?   10
If you said the computer, there are many who might   20
disagree. For example, for half a millennium books   30
were the most efficient form of written communica-   40
tions. And then there is the long-neglected art of   50
face-to-face communication, which has made way for   60
earphones, CDs, camcorders. So much for high tech!   70

1   2   3   4   5   6   7   8   9   10

Jo was given $534,789 on April 4, 1994, and $3,567   10
on June 16, 1994. This resulted in total assets of   20
$538,356. "What'll you do with so much money?" her   30
sister asked. "Oh, I guess I'll invest some in the   40
stock market, deposit some in my bank, and buy new   50
furniture with the rest." "Uh, can I ask a favor?"   60
Jo's sister Catherine asked hesitantly. "I'm broke   70
and could use a loan of $75." "Sure," Jo answered.   80

1   2   3   4   5   6   7   8   9   10

Practice	H J K L ; U I hH jJ kK lL ;: uU iI Hj Kl ;:; L K J H ; lL kK jK hH I U :; lK jH iK uU :;: A S D F G E R T aA sS dD fF gG wW eE rR tT A A S D F G E R T aA sS dD fF gG wW eE rR tT A
Words	Lisa Dirk; Fall Sail; Were;; Worth Fort Sale; Shall Lads Flask Risk True ;; Jail Slid Slide Usury Lisa Tried To Sell; Last Her House Tied Sheila Field Fried Frieda Sits Hits Fists Ask Like Sake Glide Afraid Grade Irate Lasted; As Gust Adjusted Hustler Just Jester Kiss; Faker
[Caps Lock]	Press [Caps Lock]. Type the following exercise without pressing [Shift]. LISA DIRK CALL SAIL WERE WORTH FORT SALE TO SHALL LADS FLASK TRUE JAIL SLIDE USURY SLID TRIED LISTED; WAIST ATLAS FATAL SHALL; SLAT Press [Caps Lock] again to release.
[Q] *[Q]* ↖ *[A]*	Zip [A] finger to [Q] a aa aaa q qq qqq a aa aaa q qq qqq a aa aaa a aa aaa q qq qqq a aa aaa q qq qqq a aa aaa q qq qqq a aa aaa q qq qqqaq aaqq aaq qaa qqa q qq qqq a aa aaa q qq qqqaq aaqq aaq qaa qqa aqua qua aaqq qquu ququ aqua qaqa; aq aaqq qu aqua qua aaqq qquu ququ aqua qaqa; aq aaqq qu

---

If he's elected president of the class, there will   10
be lots of changes. He's even planning a number of   20
side trips. One will be to New York City; one will   30
be to Washington, DC; one will be to Phillipsburg,   40
New Jersey; and the rest haven't been decided yet.   50

1   2   3   4   5   6   7   8   9   10

The chairman announced that seven people will have   10
to be laid off. That will create a big problem for   20
those involved because the names will be announced   30
just two days before the Christmas holiday. That's   40
a difficult time of year to initiate a job search.   50

1   2   3   4   5   6   7   8   9   10

Although spelling checkers are wonderful, they are   10
not able to distinguish between homonyms (or words   20
that sound alike) and commonly confused words. For   30
example, you would use "principle" to mean "value"   40
or "rule"; you should use the spelling "principal"   50
when you mean that something is "main" or "chief."   60

1   2   3   4   5   6   7   8   9   10

WORDS
quit quite quiet quietest last lasted:; quest
Keith Year Kirk Dirk Ukuleles: equal; equaled
rust Quit IQ: quit quite; quiet quite quitter

quit quite sight quest request sequester aqua
just quail quake equate Hearsay hither quests
little Quail Isle Aisle thirst first rest ask

[O]
[O]

   ↖

    [L]

Zip [L] finger to [O]

1 11 111 o oo ooo 1 11 111 o oo ooo 11oo 1o1o
1 11 111 o oo ooo 1 11 111 o oo ooo 11oo 1o1o

11oo 11oo oo11 1o1o o1o1 111o ooo1 111o ooo1;
11oo 11oo oo11 1o1o o1o1 111o ooo1 111o ooo1;

WORDS
loot foot food hoot route Quote quo quiet too
should fool fold Kirk look looker risk; stool
fatal goat Route Four foe Quaff just Reject::

Other oath retell tread truth Aqua saddle Ooh
lather leather other oast joust quest Request
guest lust last list lost resist sadist Ho Ho

[W]
[W]

   ↖

    [S]

Zip [S] finger to [W]

s ss sss w ww www s ss sss w ww www ss ww sws
s ss sss w ww www s ss sss w ww www ss ww sws

ss ww sws ssww ssww wwss swsw wsws ss ww swsw
ss ww sws ssww ssww wwss swsw wsws ss ww swsw

Jon had a wonderful time at the party. However, he   10
had to leave early because he had to bring the car   20
to the garage before 1:00 that evening. If not, he   30
would have had to pay an additional $9 in charges.   40

1   2   3   4   5   6   7   8   9   10

Lindsell & Sons (our big competitor) was selected.   10
"Successful Investments" was in the paper in July.   20
Her mother's a 75-year-old retired French teacher.   30
The enrollment of 350 is only half of that needed.   40

1   2   3   4   5   6   7   8   9   10

On September 21, 562 people attended the seminars.   10
I saw Mr. Goldberg on May 22, June 13, and July 5.   20
Almost 16,789,645 new people registered last year.   30
October 5 marks the 25th anniversary of the store.   40
Sally quit her job and applied for a new one here.   50

1   2   3   4   5   6   7   8   9   10

On December 15, 1992, we sent them a check for $7.   10
In 1987, six members were eligible for promotions.   20
At least 25% of the stock must be sold by April 3.   30
Check No. 21 was issued by the company last March.   40
Because he was tired, Elliot played only one game.   50

1   2   3   4   5   6   7   8   9   10

How to Take a Timed Typing and Figure Your Speed

WORDS

West wrist risk Quest; was wash washer washed
aqua tight write wrote queer quote quoter; we
Usual; Western Westerner waste stew: watered;

hid Stewart; stroke wrath wire rewire; where;
weird weirdo thought through throughout: what
whither; who whose row resod Walt Walter Welt

[P]
[P]

Zip [;] finger to [P]

↖

[;]

; ;; ;;; p pp ppp ; ;; ;;; p pp ppp ;;p pp; ;
; ;; ;;; p pp ppp ; ;; ;;; p pp ppp ;;p pp; ;

pp;; pp; ;p; pp; ;;p pp;; ;p p; ;;pp pp; ;;pp
pp;; pp; ;p; pp; ;;p pp;; ;p p; ;;pp pp; ;;pp

WORDS

Puppy equip; perk; park pot post pots; repot;
potter potted deport depart parted pester; pa
upper; Upper; dapper; flapper preppy; parade;

equip; Equipped: put puts putter putt; poise;
hope; hoped quake; parka; Parker; Pastor Will
Wipple Flower Power How; Pill Poll Pull: poet

[Y]
[Y][U]

Zip [J] finger to [Y]

↖

[J]

j jj jj y yy yy j jj jj y yy yy jj yy jj yy j
j jj jj y yy yy j jj jj y yy yy jj yy jj yy j

juy yuj jjuuyy yyuujj ju jy yuj juy jjyy juyj
juy yuj jjuuyy yyuujj ju jy yuj juy jjyy juyj

```
On Friday we should have an appointment for Arnie.    10
Josephine bought a new piano and sold the old one.    20
Janet bet fifteen dollars that her team would win.    30

1     2     3     4     5     6     7     8     9    10
```

```
T.J. Davis, the guest speaker, is a famous writer.    10
On my way here, I stopped to visit Sally and June.    20
Gracie returned the prize money she won yesterday.    30

1     2     3     4     5     6     7     8     9    10
```

```
Paul jumped when he saw the dog and cat run there.    10
Pauline Kelly worked hard to pass the examination.    20
Valerie greatly impressed the boys with her story.    30
Kyle fixed the broken chairs for Nancy and Sheila.    40

1     2     3     4     5     6     7     8     9    10
```

```
As Barbara requested, Norm will pay all the bills.    10
Jumping over the fence, she fell in the leaf pile.    20
Priscilla mixed her drink with fresh strawberries.    30
Donna was glad her family took a long summer trip.    40

1     2     3     4     5     6     7     8     9    10
```

WORDS

```
You Your Yours; Youth Petty pretty poise; yet
yet; yesterday doily putty yuppie puppy; puts
putter putty silky yellow shalt hold Yodel Ye

Hear Ye; willowy salty peppery; quilt purse::
Aye; Yes; guess Westerly: Easterly: Southerly
Disk dusk Trust topper trip warp; wrap; kites
```

Progress Check   It is time to check your progress. Please refer to Appendix A to learn how to take a timed typing and figure out your words per minute (wpm).

```
stop adjusted the hip where it rest        7
quit feasted that was there it oust       14
haul there today was after you left       21
saw a Iris dog to the old Paul door       28
she left Quaker: us in lasts yearly       35

1      2      3      4      5      6      7
_____
```

Rate Yourself   7 wpm = fair
                   14 wpm = good
                   21 wpm = very good
                   28 wpm = excellent
                   35 wpm = superior

Brain Buster #3:   *Three Consecutive Double Letters*

Name a word in the English language that has three consecutive double letters.

_____

PROGRESS CHART

Date	Total WPM	Errors	Adjusted WPM	Date	Total WPM	Errors	Adjusted WPM	Date	Total WPM	Errors	Adjusted WPM

Module 3
BOTTOM ROW KEYS

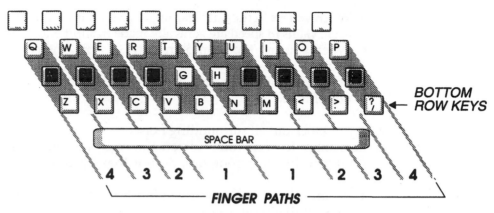

Note: Keys are spaced apart to depict finger paths

You will be moving your fingers off the home row, but they should always return to the home row.

Let's Review

Home Row

```
aa ss dd ff aa ss dd ff aa ss dd ff aa ss dd
aa ss dd ff aa ss dd ff aa ss dd ff aa ss dd

fff aaa sss ddd fff aaa sss ddd fff asdf adf
fff aaa sss ddd fff aaa sss ddd fff asdf adf

asdf asdf asdf asdf asdf asdf asdf asdf
asdf asdf asdf asdf asdf asdf asdf asdf

l ll lll ; ;; ;;; l ll lll ; ;; ;;; l ll lll
; ;; ;;; l ll lll ; ;; ;;; l ll lll ; ;; ;;;

jj kk ll ;; jj kk ll ;; jj kk ll ;; jj kk ll
;; jj kk ll ;; jj kk ll ;; jkl; jkl; jkl; kk
jkl; jkl; jkl; jkl; jkl; jkl; jkl; jk;l kl;k
```

Timing Tips

Taking a Timed Typing

1. When you are ready to begin, set a timer for 1–5 minutes, depending on your level of skill.

Hints

- When you are in the early learning stages, limit your timings to one minute each. Gains in speed are generally made in short efforts of one minutes.
- When you can type approximately 30 wpm, increase your timings to two and three minutes.
- Longer timings will help you develop the ability to type for longer periods of time.

2. Try to block out all surrounding noise.
3. Remember to keep your eyes on the copy, not on the keyboard. If you think you hit the wrong key, do not look up to verify it. Just continue typing.
4. Type until the timer rings. If you finish the timing and the timer has not rung, start that timing again.
5. Practice typing the words you misspelled.

If you have difficulty with any words or specific letters, practice them.

Home Row Words

```
all fall falls hall halls; glad Ash dash ask
lads glass Sash ALL fall falls hall; halls;;
glad ash dash gash hash glass Flask lash all
slash lads glass sash;; fall shall; gash lag
```

Home Row and Top Row Words

```
that LATH task tall tads dash had tall hall;
fat; flask flat fast; sash tads lads; sat as
flask hall halt hath GRASS lass rash ash; as
rash shalt fall fast; Last ASK sash rash rag
```

```
data date late talk lath let fatal atlas ass
sealed false feeds faded; tested raffle eggs
refused Suede auks ukulele restful true user
rest use fist Fish; gist this that risk kite
```

```
skies skit; huts rested tried:: fried hied it
rust Quit IQ: quit quite: quiet quite quitter
loot foot food hoot route Quote quo quiet too
should fool fold Kirk look looker risk; stool
```

```
whither; who whose row resod Walt Walter Welt
Wipple Flower Power How; Pill Poll Pull: poet
You Your Yours; Youth Petty pretty poise; yet
yet; yesterday doily puppy yuppie putty; puts
```

[C]
[D]

⬊

[C]

Zip [D] finger to [C]

```
d dd ddd e ee eee d dd ddd c cc ce dd ccdd
d dd ddd e ee eee d dd ddd c cc ce dd ccdd
```

```
ddcc drdc ccdd dec eecc ddcc decd ddce dc
ddcc drdc ccdd dec eecc ddcc decd ddce dc
```

```
ccdd ccddee ccddee eeddcc edc cde dec cde
ccdd ccddee ccddee eeddcc edc cde dec cde
```

Calculating Your Words Per Minute

Example of
Timed Typing

```
Pat adjusted the rig where it tore.      7
Dad adjusted the hat where it tore.     14


1     2     3     4     5     6     7
```

Words per
Minute (wpm)

Take a look at the example above. Notice that five characters—letters, spaces, and punctuation marks—count as one word. Each line on the above scale has seven words.

1. If you type the first line in one minute, you would type 7 wpm. If you type both lines in one minute, you would type 14 wpm.
2. If you complete a partial line, select the number on the scale nearest to the point at which you stopped. For example, assume you set the timer for one minute and type the following:

```
Pat adjusted the rig where it tore.
Dad adjust
```

Add the first line completed	7
to the part of the second line completed.	+2
Total	9 wpm

3. To get the adjusted wpm, deduct from your total the number of words you misspelled. (Count only one error even if the word has several incorrect letters.) That will give you the total number of correctly typed wpm.
4. If you took a timing that was for more than one minute, divide the number of minutes into your total. For example, assume you typed 60 words in 3 minutes.

$$60 \div 3 = 20 \text{ wpm}$$

WORDS

scarf call cold collar called chattel ace
scold Charles Charlie Carol Carole; Scots
scrap Pacific; specific special creed PAC

Scout race races racer raced trace traced
Crow crawls fiercest Copper Scary; DC Car
Cold Colder Coldest;; recall acquire; icy

[V]
[F]
  ↘
    [V]

Zip [F] finger to [V]

f ff ff r rr rr f ff ff c cc cc ff cc frc
f ff ff r rr rr f ff ff c cc cc ff cc frc

f ff ff c cc cc v vv vv f ff ff ff cc vv
f ff ff c cc cc v vv vv f ff ff ff cc vv

ffcc ffvv ccvv fcvf ffrr ffcc ffvv frcvf
ffcc ffvv ccvv fcvf ffrr ffcc ffvv frcvf

fff ccc vvv rrr fff ccc vvv rrr fff vvvf
fff ccc vvv rrr fff ccc vvv rrr fff vvvf

WORDS

vowel cover Voice Voiced Voiceless; veto
void avoid evade Cavern; Caverns Vacates
escape Very truly, Very truly yours, VIP

evasive evacuate evaporate Everett Evert
Value avocet avocado:: aversive; average
avid overall overly overt overtly; ovens

[B]
[F]
  ↘
[V][B]

Zip [F] finger to [B]

f ff ff r rr rr f ff ff c cc cc ff cc fc
f ff ff r rr rr f ff ff c cc cc ff cc fc

ffcc ffvv ccvv fcvf ffrr ffcc ffvv frcvf
ffcc ffvv ccvv fcvf ffrr ffcc ffvv frcvf

Appendixes

Appendix A
HOW TO TAKE A TIMED TYPING
AND FIGURE YOUR SPEED

Practice, Practice, Practice!

Before you take a timed typing, it is important to practice. Select a timing to practice. This is a wonderful way to build your speed and learn how many words per minute (wpm) you type.

First, focus on accuracy. Type the timing for one minute as fast as you can without making any errors. Circle each error you made. If you made more than two errors in the one-minute period, slow down slightly and try again. Repeat the exercise until you can type the timing with no errors.

Second, focus on speed. Type the timing as fast as you can without worrying about errors. Then, type the same timing again, pushing for a few more words per minute. Repeat this exercise until you feel you cannot type one additional word and still have your text recognizable.

Third, take the timing. Your goal is to type the timing as fast as you can without making any errors.

Note   The ["] character is used for quotation marks here, since going to the character menus will slow you down and these timings are designed to build up your speed and accuracy.

```
f ff fff v vv vvv b bb bbb fff bbb fcvbf
f ff fff v vv vvv b bb bbb fff bbb fcvbf

ff gg cc vv bb fgc vbf fgc cvb frcvb gbf
ff gg cc vv bb fgc vbf fgc cvb frcvb gbf

ccvvbb ffgg bb ffvvbb fgcvb fgcvb frgb f
ccvvbb ffgg bb ffvvbb fgcvb fgcvb frgb f
```

WORDS

```
about Bob Bobby Babble Cobbler Cable Boy
Ebb Tide: obviate obvious obtuse oboe oh
Ibis brash breach brush Brutal; brutish;

Babbitt babassu BB babushka bacillus Bad
bachelor baby blue eyes: backyard backed
backlog abrasive abvolt abyss obscured:;
```

[M]
[J]

↘

[M]

Zip [J] finger to [M]

```
j jj jjj m mm mm j jj jjj m mm mmm jmjm
j jj jjj m mm mm j jj jjj m mm mmm jmjm

jj mm jmjm jmjm mm jj jj hh mm jhm jhmj
jj mm jmjm jmjm mm jj jj hh mm jhm jhmj

jj uu jj hh jj mm juj jhj jmj juhm jumj
jj uu jj hh jj mm juj jhj jmj juhm jumj

jjmm mmjj mmhh jjuu uumm uujmm mmjuu jm
jjmm mmjj mmhh jjuu uumm uujmm mmjuu jm
```

WORDS

```
jump jumble jumbled Jack Jackass eject;
Jam James Jamie Jameson Jackson; Jesse:
object objects objected ambulate ambled

embryo obsess obsolesce oblate Obie Moe
Moth Mothy Mother Mister Miss moist Met
William Math Mathematics move moved mop
```

Bottom Row Keys   **29**

Brain Buster #15: *Traumatic Tales*

Translate the following headlines into the names of commonly known stories and fairy tales and type the names of the stories.

Example: Elderly Woman and Canine Pet Face Starvation = Old Mother Hubbard

1. Youngster Vanishes in Freak Storm

2. Couple Suffering From Dietary Allergies Reach Agreement

3. Poor Bargain Brings Ultimate Wealth

4. Friends Eager to Assist in Painting Project

5. Unique Individual Mortally Injured in Crash

6. Odd Pair Embarks on Ocean Voyage in Chartreuse Vehicle

7. Remote Country Home Vandalized by Blond

8. Browbeaten Girl Courted by Royal Heir

9. Friendless Waif Adopted by Group of Miners

10. Shepherdess Proves Derelict in Duty

Zip [S] finger to [X]

```
s  ss  ss  x  xx  xx  ss  xx  ss  xx  sx  sx  sssxx
s  ss  ss  x  xx  xx  ss  xx  ss  xx  sx  sx  sssxx

ssww  ssxx  swx  swx  xxx  sss  www  swx  sxw  x
ssww  ssxx  swx  swx  xxx  sss  www  swx  sxw  x

ssxx  ssww  swxs  swxs  ssxw  swxs  ssxw  swxs
ssxx  ssww  swxs  swxs  ssxw  swxs  ssxw  swxs

sswwxx  sssxxx  ssswxx  ssxwwx  ssxw  wsxswx
sswwxx  sssxxx  ssswxx  ssxwwx  ssxw  wsxswx
```

WORDS

Xe sexy xylan xyster xiphoid; xebec; ax
six sex Xmas sixty Exit Exist Exits axe
axis axle exact ex libris exotic exiled

exempt exhaust Exodus exogamy: exempt::
x-ray; overtax overtaxed oxygen; Oxford
Ox: X marks the spot: extreme extremely

Zip [A] finger to [Z]

```
a  aa  aaa  z  zz  zzz  aa  zz  aa  zz  aaa  zz  aa
a  aa  aaa  z  zz  zzz  aa  zz  aa  zz  aaa  zz  aa

aazz  aaqq  aazz  aaqq  qaz  zaq  qaz  azz  zqq
aazz  aaqq  aazz  aaqq  qaz  zaq  qaz  azz  zqq

zzza  aaaq  qqqa  aaaz  zaqa  azaq  qaza  aqzz
zzza  aaaq  qqqa  aaaz  zaqa  azaq  qaza  aqzz

qqaazz  zzaaqq  qqzzaa  aazzqq  qaz  zaq  qaz
qqaazz  zzaaqq  qqzzaa  aazzqq  qaz  zaq  qaz
```

Timed Typings

Programming languages, as spoken languages, take a	10
variety of forms. For instance, the language C was	20
developed by Bell Labs as a compiler language. And	30
BASIC is a high-level interactive language used in	40
systems that have data communication capabilities.	50
In RPG II you have a problem-oriented language for	60
generating reports; with COBOL you have a language	70
that uses vocabulary spoken in the business world.	80

1   2   3   4   5   6   7   8   9   10

It is vital that you type computer languages with-	10
out any mistakes because any spelling error can be	20
read by the computer as an error and can cause the	30
program to end with an error message. Also, if you	40
put a decimal in the wrong place, it would be just	50
as if you put it in the wrong location on a check.	60

1   2   3   4   5   6   7   8   9   10

WORDS

Zebra Quiz Quizzes Quizzed Azores: Zest
ooze oozed oozes zygomatic Zealot Zaire
ZAP: zinc Aztec azalea azure maze amaze

matzo ball; maximize; hazards; buzzard;
Mazurka iodize oxidize Zeisler: Zimmer:
Zurich; Zeya; Zambia; Zab zoo doze daze

[N]
  [J]
  ↙
[N][M]

Zip [J] finger to [N]

j jj jjj m mm mmm j jj jjj n nn nnn jnj
j jj jjj m mm mmm j jj jjj n nn nnn jnj

jjmm jjnn jjmn jjnm mmnn jmnj nnjj jnmj
jjmm jjnn jjmn jjnm mmnn jmnj nnjj jnmj

jjhh jjuu jjmm jjnn jumn jhnm jjmmnn jn
jjhh jjuu jjmm jjnn jumn jhnm jjmmnn jn

jjmmjjm mmjjmmj jjnmjjn mjnm jmmj mnnjm
jjmmjjm mmjjmmj jjnmjjn mjnm jmmj mnnjm

WORDS

Nancy Nannette; ennoble enough narcotic
Nation; Indian: natron natural network:
response responsive responsiveness next

panniers staunches; Norton N. Nicholson
Nelson; niceness piano picnic; Jacobean
itinerant converts conversion announces

You have now learned the entire alphabet. Type it until you are comfortable
with all the letters.

Alphabet

a b c d e f g h i j k l m n o p q r s t u v w x y z

ab cd ef gh ij kl mn op qr st uv wx yz
abc def ghi jkl mno pqr stu vwx yz

```
        (error 'parse-proc "( expected")
        (parse-variable*-rparen-exp  '() (rest item-stream) receiver))))

(define parse-variable*-rparen-exp
  (lambda (vars-so-far item-stream receiver)
    (if (eq? (lexical-item->class (first item-stream))
             'rparen)
        ;; if no more variables, send on an answer to a procedure
        ;; that puts the body (an <exp>) in it.
        (parse-exp
         (rest item-stream)
         (lambda (body unused-items)
           (receiver (make-proc vars-so-far body)
                     unused-items)))
        ;; otherwise add one more name to the list of variables
        (let* ((v-item (first item-stream))
               (class  (lexical-item->class v-item))
               (data   (lexical-item->data  v-item)))
          (if (not (eq? class 'variable))
              (error 'parse-proc "Variable expected: at ~s" v-item)
              ;; add name to list; call again
              (parse-variable*-rparen-exp
                 (append vars-so-far (list data))
                 (rest item-stream)
                 receiver))))))))


;  _____
;; Look at a typical one of these procedures:
;;   notice: 1.) making the tree
;;           2.) the continuation-passing style

;; the rest of an assignment-expression
;;    assign-sym <exp>

(define parse-assign
  (lambda (var item-stream receiver)
    (if (not (eq?
```

Aa Bb Cc Dd Ee Ff Gg Hh Ii Jj Kk Ll Mm
Nn Oo Pp Qq Rr Ss Tt Uu Vv Ww Xx Yy Zz

Index Fingers   Your index fingers type approximately 46 percent of the letters of the alphabet. Let's practice using your index fingers only.

fur gun gum fun hut hum but buy jut bug bun
fur gun gum fun hut hum but buy jut bug bun

guy hung hug bunt hunt gnu grunt fry guru
guy hung hug bunt hunt gnu grunt fry guru

Progress Check   It is time to check your progress once again. If you have not gotten much faster since the last module, do not worry. You are still very much in the learning stage.

about	beat	card	debit	enough	feisty	7
gamma	hard	ibis	knife	laughs	mister	14
newer	open	pins	quite	really	spouse	21
tried	unit	very	woman	xyloid	yearly	28
zebra	quit	want	paper	loiter	crayon	35

1   2   3   4   5   6   7

pencils	paper	scissors	glue	erasers	7
spinach	lettuce	radish	tomato	beans	14
comma	period	semicolon	quote	hyphen	21
New York	Arkansas	Washington	Kansas		28
dress	skirt	pants	blouse	scarf ring	35

1   2   3   4   5   6   7

Rate Yourself   7 wpm = fair
14 wpm = good
21 wpm = very good
28 wpm = excellent
35 wpm = superior

```
    r1=0;  r2=0;  r3=0;  r4=0;

    for(loop=0;loop <= 10;  ++loop){
     nextbit = (( buffer >> loop) & 1);
     temp = r4;
     r4 = r3;
     r3 = r2;
     r2 = r1 ^ temp;
     r1 = nextbit ^ temp;}

    buffer ^= ( (r1 << 14) ^ (r2 << 13) ^ (r3 << 12) ^ (r4 << 11) );

    if( shift == 16){
     shift=1;
     buffer1 = buffer << shift;
     *(file2 + (count++)) = buffer1;}
```

LISP

```
(define parse-decl
  (lambda (item-stream receiver)
    (let ((var-part (first item-stream)))
    (if (not (eq?
               (lexical-item->class var-part)
               'variable))
        (error 'parse-decl "Variable expected: at ~s" var-part)
        (let ((equals-part (rest item-stream)))
          (if (not (eq?
                     (lexical-item->class (first equals-part))
                     'equal-sign))
              (error 'parse-decl "= expected: at ~s" (first equals-part))
              (parse-exp
               (rest equals-part)
               (lambda (exp unused-items)
                 (receiver (make-decl
                            (lexical-item->data var-part)
                            exp) unused-items)))))))))

;; the rest of a proc-expression
;;   lparen { <variable> }* rparen <exp>

(define parse-proc
  (lambda (item-stream receiver)
    (if (not (eq?
               (lexical-item->class (first item-stream))
               'lparen))
```

Brain Buster #4:   *Consecutive Vowels*

Think of words that have three, four, and five consecutive vowels.

1. Three consecutive vowels _____

2. Four consecutive vowels _____

3. Five consecutive vowels _____

C

```
/******          Simulate shift register          ******/

    r1=0; r2=0; r3=0; r4=0;

    for(loop=0;loop <= 10; ++loop){
      nextbit = (( buffer >> loop) & 1);
      temp = r4;
      r4 = r3;
      r3 = r2;
      r2 = r1 ^ temp;
      r1 = nextbit ^ temp;}


/******          Logically or message & parity digits    ******/

    buffer ^= ( (r1 << 14) ^ (r2 << 13) ^ (r3 << 12) ^ (r4 << 11) );

    if(overflow == 0)
      left  = 16 - (11 - left);
    else
     if(overleft == 50)
      overflow = 0

    prev = cond;

/******          Do bit manipulation in 16 bit buffer       ******/

    if( shift == 16){
      shift=1;
      buffer1 = buffer << shift;}
    else{
      buffer1 ^= buffer >> (15-shift);
      ++shift;

      *(file2 + (count++)) = buffer1;

      buffer1 = 0;
      buffer1 |= buffer << shift;}}}

/*******   After all data read in, are there stray bits? (i.e. is file in
        bytes modulus 16 = 0?                               *******/

 if(left !=0){
   buffer=0;
   buffer ^= prev << 11-left;
   buffer &= 003777;
```

Module 4
PUNCTUATION MARKS

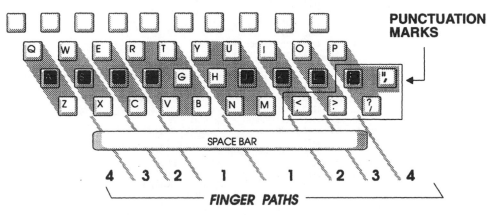

PUNCTUATION MARKS

FINGER PATHS

Note: Keys are spaced apart to depict finger paths

Now that you have learned the entire alphabet, it is time to type sentences. But what is a sentence without punctuation marks?

[;]   You have already learned the semicolon. It is a home row key. Let's just practice.

Note   Space once after a semicolon.

```
Atlanta, Georgia; Nyack, New York; Taos, New
Mexico; Dallas, Texas; Louisville, Kentucky;
San Francisco, California; Phoenix, Arizona;

Tuesday, January 9; Monday, April 3; Friday,
July 7; Thursday, November 9; Saturday, May,
20; Wednesday, February 8; Sunday, August 27
```

[.]
[L]   Zip [L] finger to [.]

  ↘
    [.]

```
1 11 111 . .. ... 11.. ..11 1..1 .11. 11 ...
1 11 111 . .. ... 11.. ..11 1..1 .11. 11 ...
```

```
         58   52     D1   034D  343            Cmpl     R2,R8                 ;Compare Amt.checked to Si
              F0     15   0350  344            Bleq     Compare               ;If <= Then goto Compare
                          0352  345
              59     D4   0352  346 NotFound:  Clrl     R9                    ;Else Set R9 to Zero
    59  FFFFFFFF 8F  D0   0354  347            Movl     #-1,R9                ;Move -1 to R9
              04        035B  348            Ret                            ;Return
                          035C  349
              59     01   D0   035C  350 Found:     Movl     #1,R9                 ;Move 1 to R9
              04        035F  351            Ret                            ;Return
                          0360  352                     $EXIT_S  Lokup
                          036A  353 ;(**********************************************************************)
                          036A  354
                   4000   036A  355                     .Entry Assign3, ^M<IV>
                          036C  356
              53     D4   036C  357            Clrl     R3                    ;Clear the Prog Ctr.
    53  00000000'EF  DE   036E  358            MovAl    A1000,R3              ;Move Addr. Line 1
                          0375  359
                          0375  360 NextLine:
              57     D4   0375  361            Clrl     R7                    ;Clear Register 7
              54     D4   0377  362            Clrl     R4                    ;Clear Register 4
              54  83  90  0379  363            Movb     (R3)+, R4             ;Move Opcode to R4
58 00000320 8F FFFFFFFF 8F C1 037C 364         Addl3    #-1,#TabSize,R8       ;Move Offset to R8
              56  FC74 CF DE  0388  365            Moval    Table,R6              ;Move Table to R6
         AF  AF   02   F3   038D  366            Calls    #2, Lokup             ;Look for Target
                          0391  367
                          0391  368
              59     D5   0391  369            Tstl     R9                    ;Test Register 9
              06     14   0393  370            Bgtr     Foundit               ;If R9>0 Goto Foundit
                          0395  371
         000005A0'EF  17  0395  372            Jmp      Error                 ;Else Goto End
                          039B  373
                          039B  374 Foundit:
         B1  AF   06   D0   039B  375            Movl     #word_size, Size      ;Move Wrd-Size to Size
              FF7D CF  DF   039F  376            Pushal   Size                  ;Push Size on Stack
              01  A6   DF   03A3  377            Pushal   1(R6)                 ;Push Addr. of String
    00000000'EF  02   FB   03A6  378            Calls    #2, Write_String      ;Write String
                          03AD  379
              00     54   91   03AD  380            Cmpb     R4,#^X00              ;If Opcode=Halt Exit
              06     12   03B0  381            Bneq     Okay                  ;Else goto okay
         000005A0'EF  17  03B2  382            Jmp      Done
                          03B8  383
    FF7B CF    07  A6   90   03B8  384 Okay:      Movb     7(R6),NumOper         ;Get # of Operands
         00  FF77 CF   91   03BE  385            Cmpb     NumOper,#0            ;Compare NumOps to 0
              15     12   03C3  386            Bneq     HasOps                ;If not = goto hasops
    00000001 8F    DF   03C5  387            Pushal   #1                    ;Else Push 1 on Stack
         FF60 CF    DF   03CB  388            Pushal   Spayce                ;Push Space on stack
    00000000'EF  02   F3   03CF  389            Calls    #2,Write_String_Cr    ;Do a Carriage Ret.
              53     96   03D6  390            Incb     R3                    ;Get Next byte
              9B     11   03D8  391            Brb      NextLine              ;goto nextline
                          03DA  392
              52     D4   03DA  393 HasOps:    Clrl     R2                    ;Clear Register 2
              52     01   C0   03DC  394            Addl2    #1,R2                 ;Increment Index
                          03DF  395
              58     D4   03DF  396 Loop5:     Clrl     R8                    ;Clear Register 8
              57     D4   03E1  397            Clrl     R7                    ;Clear Register 7
 FF55 CF  63  F0 8F  8B   03E3  398            Bicb3    #^XF0,(R3),Lower      ;Move lower 4 bits
         57  FF51 CF  90   03EA  399            Movb     Lower,R7
```

```
lloo ll.. llo. ..lo ool. ll.. ...o 11.1 ol..
lloo ll.. llo. ..lo ool. ll.. ...o 11.1 ol..
```

Abbreviations

```
Dr. A.M.A. Jr. Sr. Mr. Mrs. Ms. Esq. St. Rd.
Ave. doz. lb. Inc. Ltd. Rev. Msgr. A.M. P.M.
B.A. B.S. M.A. M.S. M.B.A. Ph.D. e.g.; i.e.;
```

Sentences

Note

Space once after a period at the end of a sentence.

```
Sam fed us. See Mr Doe. Lou asked for salad.
Bob sold all his dogs. Dale saw the cowboys.
He did. She did. Yes. Janice wrote a letter.
```

```
I have learned to type. He types quite well.
Eve used a computer. The ski slope is steep.
I like the color yellow. I also like purple.
```

[,]
[K]
  ↘
  [,]

Zip [K] finger to [,]

```
k kk kkk , ,, ,,, kk,, ,,kk k,,k ,kk, kk ,,,
k kk kkk , ,, ,,, kk,, ,,kk k,,k ,kk, kk ,,,
```

```
kkii kk,, kki, ,,ki iik, kk,, ,,,,i kk,k ik,,
kkii kk,, kki, ,,ki iik, kk,, ,,,,i kk,k ik,,
```

Words

Note

Space once after a comma.

```
, happy, glad, mad, elated, Spanish, French,
Spanish, story, video, computer, television,
cereal, crackers, zesty, panic, work, works,
evenly, commas, comas, comes, type, end, , ,
```

```
121    C*
122    CSR                    SETOF                              010221
123    CSR                    SETOF                              2999
124    C*
125    CSR                    MOVE DATE          DATE IN 60
126    CSR                    MOVE DATEIN        YR      20         YEAR
127    CSR                    MOVELDATEIN        MONTH   20         MONTH
128    CSR                    MOVE DATEIN        DAYYR   40         DAY/YEAR
129    CSR                    MOVELDATEYR        DAY     20         DAY
130    CSR                    MOVELDATEIN        MTHDAY  40         MONTH/DAY
131    C*
132    CSR        MONTH       COMP 01                        01    01HIGH/EQ
133    CSR 01     MONTH       COMP 12                        0101LOW/EQ
134    CSRNO1                 SETON                          99    ERROR
135    CSRNO1 99              GOTO ENDAT
136    C*
137    CSR                    SETOF                          01
138    CSR        DAY         COMP 01                        01    01HIGH/EQ
139    CSR 01     DAY         COMP 31                        0101LOW/EQ
140    CSRNO1                 SETON                              99
141    CSRNO1 99              GOTO ENDAT
142    C*
143    CSR        UYEAR       ADD  1             YRPLS   20         YEAR PLUS1
144    CSR        UYEAR       SUB  1             YRLES   20         YEAR LESS1
145    CSR        YR          COMP YRLES                         02
146    CSRNO2     YR          COMP UYEAR                         02
147    CSRNO2     YR          COMP YRPLS                         02
148    CSRNO2                 SETON                          99
149    CSRNO2 99              GOTO ENDAT
150    C*
151    CSR        YR          DIV  4             LEAP    10
152    CSR                    MVR                LEAP2   10         21 EQ ZEROES.
153    CSR        MTHDAY      COMP 0229                          29EQ
154    CSR 21 29              GOTO ENDAT                              GOOD LEAP YEAR
155    CSRN21 29              SETON                          99    ERROR
156    CSR 99                 GOTO ENDAT
157    C*
158    CSR        MTHDAY      COMP 0230                          99EQ  FEB
159    CSRN99     MTHDAY      COMP 0231                          99EQ  FEB
160    CSRN99     MTHDAY      COMP 0431                          99EQ  APRIL
161    CSRN99     MTHDAY      COMP 0631                          99EQ  JUNE
162    CSRN99     MTHDAY      COMP 0931                          99EQ  SEPTEMBER
163    CSRN99     MTHDAY      COMP 1131                          99EQ  NOVEMBER
164    C*
165    CSR        ENDAT       ENDSR
166    C************************************************
167    0REPORT T 202     L1
168    0                                 9 'AR0005.01'
169    0                                77 'G.C.C. BEVERAGES, INC.'
170    0                               122 'PAGE'
171    0                       PAGE  Z  127
172    0          T 2     11
173    0                                 6 'BRANCH'
174    0                       BRANCH    11
175    0                       BRNAME    33
176    0                               122 'DATE'
177    0                       UDATE Y  132
178    0                                68 'EMPLOYEE RECEIVABLES'
179    0                                83 'CONTROL TOTALS'
180    0          T 2     L1
```

Sentences	Yes, he did. No, he will not. Try it, Ginny.
	Please, Barbara. No, I cannot. Okay, I will.
	Later, perhaps. Good, we can. Yes, tomorrow.

Okay, it is finished. No, it is not snowing.
Try it, Edward. Eat it, Susan. No, I cannot.
If it is, I will. However, I will see later.

[:]

The colon appears above the semicolon on a home row key. Leave your finger on the semicolon and press [Shift] with your pinky to type a colon.

```
; ;; ;;; : :: ::: ;; :: ;;; ::: ;:; ::; ;;:;
; ;; ;;; : :: ::: ;; :: ;;; ::: ;:; ::; ;;:;
```

Words

Note

Space once after a colon.

Ladies: Gentlemen: Dear Ms. Smith: From: To:
Ladies and Gentlemen: the following: follow:

To Whom This May Concern: as follows: Mommy:
Dear Mr. Quincy: Dear Judge Williams: Hello:

Sentences

I like the following fruits: apples, grapes,
and strawberries.
The following names were listed: Mr. Matson,
Mrs. Kirk, and Ms. Fallon.
Please take the following: tent, stoves, and
matches.

[']
[;] → [']

Zip [;] finger to [']

```
; ;; ;;; ' '' ''' ; ;; ;;; ' '' ''' ; ;; '''
; ;; ;;; ' '' ''' ; ;; ;;; ' '' ''' ; ;; '''
```

```
17.9                           MOVE "T" TO DATE-MISMATCH-FLAG
18                      ELSE
18.1                        IF PROCESS-DAY NOT = RA-SETTLEMENT-DAY
18.2                            MOVE "T" TO DATE-MISMATCH-FLAG
18.3                        ELSE
18.4                            PERFORM C003-READ-RASYS-FILE
18.5                ELSE
18.6                    PERFORM C003-READ-RASYS-FILE.
18.7        B002-MAIN-PROCEDURE-EXIT.    EXIT.
18.8
18.9

19          C002-READ-DATE-FILE.
19.1            READ PROCESS-DATE-FILE.
19.2              IF PROCESS-DATE-FILE-STAT NOT = "00"
19.3                  MOVE PROCESS-DATE-FILE-STAT TO KSAM-FILE-STATUS
19.4                  MOVE "Y" TO ANY-KSAM-ERRORS
19.5                  MOVE "READ" TO KSAM-FILE-OPER
19.6                  MOVE "WORKFILE" TO KSAM-FILE-NAME
19.7                  PERFORM KSAM-ERROR-ROUTINE.
19.8        C002-READ-DATE-FILE-EXIT.    EXIT.
19.9
20
20.1

20.2        C003-READ-RASYS-FILE.
20.3            READ SYSTEM-CONTROL-FILE.
20.4            IF NOT RA-END-OF-FILE
20.5              IF SYS-CNTRL-STAT NOT = "00"
20.6                  MOVE SYS-CNTRL-STAT TO KSAM-FILE-STATUS
20.7                  MOVE "Y" TO ANY-KSAM-ERRORS
```

Words

Note   Do not space after an apostrophe unless it ends a word.

```
won't can't didn't wasn't haven't hadn't A's
Mr. Jones' sister-in-law's dog's dogs' wit's
```

Sentences
```
Samuel Jones was at his wit's end yesterday.
The ladies' and men's locker rooms are here.
The Cohens' house is just across the street.

Their horses' stalls were cleaned yesterday.
The audience's reaction was very astounding.
The new children's books are in that corner.
```

["]   Zip [;] to ['] and press [Shift]

User Manual   This key is commonly used for quoted material, but you should refer to your User Manual for instructions on how to type professional-looking quotation marks. Reserve the ["] key for inches (as in dimensions) or minutes (as in latitude and longitude).]

```
; ;; ;; ' '' ''' " "" """ ;; '' "" ;'" ;'""
; ;; ;; ' '' ''' " "" """ ;; '' "" ;'" ;'""
```

[?]
[;]

  ↘
    [?]

```
; ;; ;;; ? ?? ??? ;;?? ??;; ;??; ?;;? ;; ???
; ;; ;;; ? ?? ??? ;;?? ??;; ;??; ?;;? ;; ???
```

Words

Note   Space once after a question mark.

```
Who? How? Why? When? Did you? Did he? Maybe?
Can she? Why not? If not now, when? Did she?
Will she? Can we? Did they? Could they? Huh?
```

```
330 PRINT
340 PRINT "TOTAL GUESTS FOR LUXURY HOTEL:";TL
350 PRINT
360 PRINT "TOTAL GUESTS FOR MODERATE HOTEL:";TM
370 PRINT
380 LET DL=TL*75.00
390 LET DM=TM*50.00
```

COBOL

```
14.7               STOP RUN.
14.8
14.9
15           B000-HOUSEKEEPING.
15.1
15.2             OPEN INPUT PROCESS-DATE-FILE.
15.3             IF PROCESS-DATE-FILE-STAT NOT = "00"
15.4                MOVE PROCESS-DATE-FILE-STAT TO KSAM-FILE-STATUS
15.5                MOVE "Y" TO ANY-KSAM ERRORS
15.6                MOVE "OPEN" TO KSAM-FILE-OPER
15.7                MOVE "WORKFILE" TO KSAM-FILE-NAME
15.8                PERFORM KSAM-ERROR-ROUTINE.
15.9
16
16.1             OPEN INPUT SYSTEM-CONTROL-FILE.
16.2             IF SYS-CNTRL-STAT NOT = "00"
16.3                MOVE SYS-CNTRL-STAT TO KSAM-FILE-STATUS
16.4                MOVE "Y" TO ANY-KSAM-ERRORS
16.5                MOVE "OPEN" TO KSAM-FILE-OPER
16.6                MOVE "RASYSCNT" TO KSAM-FILE-NAME
16.7                PERFORM KSAM-ERROR-ROUTINE.
16.8
16.9             PERFORM C002-READ-DATE-FILE.
17               PERFORM C003-READ-RASYS-FILE.
17.1       B000-HOUSEKEEPING EXIT.    EXIT.
17.2
17.3
17.4
17.5
17.6       B002-MAIN-PROCEDURE.
17.7             IF RASYSCNT-REC-ID = "RA"
17.8                IF PROCESS-MONTH NOT = RA-SETTLEMENT-MONTH
```

Do you know? Did they ask? Will you ask her?
Does he think so? Why was he not also asked?

[/]
[;]
↘
[/]

Zip [;] finger to [/]

The virgule is known by many names, including *diagonal, solidus, oblique, slant, slash,* and *slash mark.* It is generally used to represent a word that is not written out or to separate or set off certain adjacent elements of text.

The virgule can also be used for computer applications. It should not be confused with the back slash [\], used frequently in computer commands and file names.

; ;; ; ? ?? ??? / // /// ; // ??? ? ;; ///?/
; ;; ; ? ?? ??? / // /// ; // ??? ? ;; ///?/

Note

Do not space after a virgule.

Send the package c/o Sally Reynolds.
The A/V room will open at nine tomorrow.
Ms. Smith and/or Mr. Jones will be there.
They estimated 40,000 tons/year.

The projectile traveled 9 ft/sec.
I received an I/O error on the computer.
What is the price/earnings ratio?
The article is in the May/June issue.
It was in 1990/91.
It is an innovative classroom/laboratory.

[-]
↗ [-]
[P]
↗
[;]

Zip [;] finger to [-] (This is a big Zip.)

; ;; - -- --- ; ;; ;;; p pp ppp - -- ---
; ;; - -- --- ; ;; ;;; p pp ppp - -- ---

```
4100 IF Q$="Y" THEN LSET BN$=N$:PUT #1, R ELSE 4005
4110 RETURN
5000 '***********  NOT FOUND ROUTINE
5010 CLS
5020 PRINT"LICENSE NUMBER NOT ON FILE"
5030 FOR X=1 TO 1000: NEXT X
5040 RETURN
```

BASIC (Exercise 2)

```
10 TRAVEL ARRANGEMENTS
20 CHRISTA BAYER 8/2/83
30 PROGRAM CALCULATES NUMBER OF GUESTS FOR LUXURY
40 AND MODERATE HOTELS. IT ALSO DETERMINES AMOUNT
50 OF DEPOSIT TO BE SENT TO EACH HOTEL.
60 *****INITIALIZATION
70 CLS
80 CLEAR 500
90 LET DL=0
100 LET DM=0
110 LET E1$="%(18TO)%(20TO)%TO%"
120 *****DATA DICTIONARY
130 G$ GUEST
140 H$ HOTEL
150 TL TOTAL GUESTS FOR LUXURY HOTEL
160 TM TOTAL GUESTS FOR MODERATE HOTEL
170 DL DEPOSIT FOR LUXURY HOTEL
180 DM DEPOSIT FOR MODERATE HOTEL
190 *****HEADINGS
200 PRINT TAB(21);"TRAVEL ARRANGEMENTS"
210 PRINT STRING$(64,"=")
220 PRINT TAB(5);"GUEST";TAB(40);"HOTEL"
230 PRINT STRING$(64,"-")
240 READ G$,H$
250 DATA "GAITHER,SUSAN",LUX,"AMOS,BOB",MOD
260 DATA "WILLIAMS,RAE",MOD,"WHITE,WILL",LUX
270 DATA "ARGO,HELEN",LUX,"EOD",EOD
280 IF G$="EOD" THEN 330
290 PRINT USING E1$;G$,H$
300 IF H$="LUX" THEN TL=TL+1
310 IF H$="MOD" THEN TM=TM+1
320 GOTO 240
```

Note

Do not space after a hyphen.

```
mayor-elect write-in trade-in write-off
sister-in-law H-beam A-frame J-bar lift
off-season rates stick-to-itiveness A-C
```

Sentences

```
He just got a part-time job.
It was a very well-funded project.
The man next door is a jack-of-all-trades.
```

```
The president is a tough-minded negotiator.
The contract has an iron-clad guarantee.
Do not worry, it is a risk-free investment.
```

[!]
[!]

[Q]

[A]

Zip [A] finger to [1] and press [Shift]

```
a aa aaa q qq qqq 1 11 ! !! !!! 11!! !!11
a aa aaa q qq qqq 1 11 ! !! !!! 11!! !!11
```

```
aaa qqq 111 !!! !!! 111 qqq aaa aq1 1qa!!
aaa qqq 111 !!! !!! 111 qqq aaa aq1 1qa!!
```

Words

Note

Space once after an exclamation point.

```
No, no! Ugh! Fire! Stop! Stop that! Ouch!
Wow! Alas! The time is now! Eek! A mouse!
Wait! Absurd! Yes, yes! Get out! Not now!
```

Sentences

```
What an awful time we had!
Sh! The meeting has begun.
Psst! Come over here.
```

BASIC (Exercise 1)

```
10  'RCHANGE
20  'CHRISTA BAYER 08/23/83
30  'PROGRAM CHANGES A RECORD ON FILE
40  '************   DATA DICTIONARY
50  'L$...... LICENSE NUMBER ...INPUT
60  'BL$..... BUFFER LICENSE NUMBER
70  'N$...... NEW NAME ...INPUT
80  'BN$..... BUFFER NAME
1000 '*********   CONTROL MODULE
1010 CLEAR 2000
1020 GOSUB 2000
1030 PRINT"ENTER LICENSE NO. OR END"
1040 LINE INPUT L$
1050 IF L$="END" THEN CLOSE #1: END ELSE GOSUB 3000
1060 GOTO 1030
2000 '*********   INITIALIZATION
2005 CLS
2010 POKE 16916,2
2020 PRINT"CHANGES NAME ON RECORD OF DRIVERS LICENSE"
2025 PRINT
2030 OPEN "R",1,"CBRFILE"
2040 FIELD #1,1 AS B1$,15 AS BL$,20 AS BN$
2050 RETURN
3000 '***********   SEARCH
3010 LET R=1
3020 GET #1,R
3030 IF L$=BL$ THEN GOSUB 4000: RETURN
3040 LET R=R+1
3050 IF EOF(1) THEN GOSUB 5000: RETURN
3060 GOTO 3020
4000 '*************   FOUND ROUTINE
4005 CLS
4010 PRINT"ENTER NEW NAME"
4020 LINE INPUT N$
4030 CLS
4040 PRINT"FORMER NAME:    ";BN$
4050 PRINT
4060 PRINT"NEW NAME:       ";N$
4070 PRINT
4080 PRINT"IS NEW NAME CORRECT"
4090 LINE INPUT Q$
```

Ouch! That hurts.
Ugh! What a horrible taste.
Ah, those blue eyes!

[( )]   Zip [L] finger to [9] and press [Shift] for a left parenthesis.
[( )]   Zip [;] finger to [0] and press [Shift] for a right parenthesis.
  ↖ ↖
[O] [P]

  ↖   ↖   1 11 111 o oo ooo 9 99 999 ((((((lo9((9ol
[L] [;]   1 11 111 o oo ooo 9 99 999 ((((((lo9((9ol

           ; ;; ;;; p pp ppp 0 00 000)))))) 0p;))p;0
           ; ;; ;;; p pp ppp 0 00 000)))))) 0p;))p;0

Words

Note   Do not space after a left parenthesis; space once after a right parenthesis.

           (left)(right)(parentheses)(open)(close)
           (not brackets)(wow)(big)(help)(enclose)
           (shout)(he thought)(she wants)(wishful)

Sentences Please call Evelyn (by telephone) tomorrow.
           Please designate the exact Road (or Rd).
           Antonyms (such as pro, con) are opposites.

           Have you heard of Earl (Fatha) Hines?
           I'll know more later tomorrow (Friday).
           The diagram (next page) illustrates that.

Module 14
COMPUTER LANGUAGES _____

Computers, as well as humans, use language(s) to communicate. And computers, as well as humans, communicate in different languages. Programming languages take many forms and are used for a variety of purposes.

BASIC   [*B*eginners' *A*ll-Purpose *S*ymbolic *I*nstruction *C*ode] An interactive means of communication used in systems that have data communication capabilities. BASIC is a high-level language that has alphabetic and numeric capabilities.

COBOL   [*C*ommon *B*usiness-*O*riented *L*anguage] A self-documenting language that uses the vocabulary of the business world because it is much like the English language. It also has alphabetic and numeric capabilities.

RPG II   [*R*eport *P*rogram *G*enerator *II*] A problem-oriented language, used primarily to generate business reports.

Assembly   A program called Assembler translates Assembly programs into machine code. With this program you can *talk* to your computer in its own language.

C   A compiler language developed by Bell Laboratories. It is the language in which UNIX was written and can handle conditions that are written in Assembly language.

LISP   [*L*ist *P*rocessor] A language used in mathematical research and artificial intelligence. It manipulates symbols and is used to handle strings of information that are known as lists.

The Importance of Accuracy   Accuracy is imperative when typing any computer language. The slightest typographical error might cause the program to terminate with an error message. Think of the consequences if you debit $100 instead of $1,000 in your checkbook or you send a letter to Ms. Smith instead of Mr. Smith.

Type the following exercises exactly as they appear. If you were a computer programmer typing these exercises for a real-world application, you would not use a word processor; rather, you would enter the data directly into the system. So, spell checkers are not available. Check your work very carefully.

It is time to check your progress once again. If you have not gotten much faster since the last module, do not worry. These are slightly more difficult.

```
Yes, she ordered the A/V equipment.      7
"How," he asked, "are you feeling?"      14
Kelly called her new mother-in-law.      21
Dan Jones ordered the following: an      28
ice-cream cone and a tuna sandwich.      35
```

1	2	3	4	5	6	7

```
He liked the blue Chevy in the lot.      7
Carol bought the red couch on sale.      14
Steve asked, "What were the costs?"      21
David received his M.B.A. from MIT.      28
He called her from Aspen, Colorado.      35
```

1	2	3	4	5	6	7

Rate Yourself   7 wpm = fair
14 wpm = good
21 wpm = very good
28 wpm = excellent
35 wpm = superior

Punctuation Marks

Brain Buster #14: *Simply Stated*

Reduce the following into commonly used expressions and type those expressions.

Example: A gyrating lithoidal fragment never accrues lichen. = A rolling stone gathers no moss.

1. Similar sire, similar scion.
2. Tenants of vitreous abodes ought not hurl lithoidal fragments.
3. It is not proper for mendicants to be indicative of preference.
4. It is fruitless to become lacrimatory because of scattered lacteal fluid.
5. Pulchritude does not extend below the surface of the derma.
6. Every article that is coruscated is not fashioned from aureate metal.
7. Freedom from guile or fraud constitutes the most excellent procedure.
8. Consolidated, you and I maintain ourselves; separated, we defer to the law of gravity.
9. You cannot estimate the contents of a bound printed narrative of record from the exterior vesture.
10. A feathered creature clasped in the manual member is equal in value to a brace in the bosky growth.

Brain Buster #5: Oxymorons

The term *oxymoron* goes back to a Greek word that combines *oxus,* "sharp," and *moros,* "foolish," and means "pointedly foolish." Thus an oxymoron is a term that contradicts itself. Type each sentence and complete it, supplying the second word of a commonly used oxymoron.

Example: That went over like a lead <u>balloon.</u>

1. The music was recorded _____ in the studio.

2. The Democrats mounted loyal _____ to the bill.

3. The report showed a standard _____ of 15 percent.

4. Do you think our criminal _____ system is working?

5. She is a student _____ at Hawkins Elementary School.

6. We'll be using plastic _____ for the picnic.

7. Please arrange the files alphabetically; they are now in random _____.

8. That picture is awful. In fact, it's pretty _____.

9. Lincoln was alive during the Civil _____.

10. That happened last week; it's old _____.

EXERCISE 4

Sorting

```
$ sort people > people1
$ sort +1 people > people 2
$ comm people1 people 2
Bob Littlehale   100
Beth Wolf        122
Donna Randall    114
Frank Nelson     112
Miche Grenier    120
Dick Tucker      121
John Carpenter   101
Jim Edwards      113
C. Cucurillo     111
Jim Greene       110
$
```

EXERCISE 5

Calendars

```
$ cat calendar
Tuesday, Feb. 11 - Jon's birthday
Tuesday, Feb. 4 - shop for Jon's present
2/15 classes start, 8-8:30 pm
Friday 217 dentist appt. - 4 pm
Saturday at 8 for mystery dinner
$
```

Module 5
NUMBERS AND SYMBOLS

When you type numbers, you have the option of using the numbers on the keyboard or those on the numeric keypad. It is strictly your preference based on ease of use and/or speed. Please note, however, that there are no symbols over the numbers on the numeric keypad. This module will focus on the numbers on the keyboard and their associated symbols. For more information on the numeric keypad, please refer to Module 6.

When you want to type a symbol that appears above a number on the keyboard, press [Shift], just as you would for a capital letter. Keyboards usually include any or all of the following symbols:

!   exclamation mark
@   at
#   number
$ dollar(s)
%   percent
^   caret
&   ampersand
*   asterisk
=   equal sign
+   plus sign

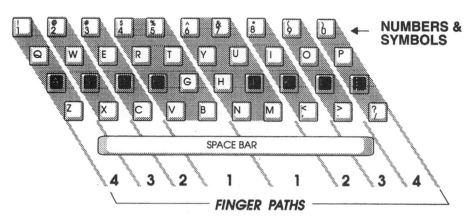

Note: Keys are spaced apart to depict finger paths

```
$ ls
a            aA           aB           aC           c1
c10          c11          c12          c13          c2
c3           c4           c5           c6           c7
c8           c9           contents     f1-1         f10-1
f11-1        f11-2        f2-1         f2-2         f2-3
f7-1         f8-1         f8-2         t3-1         t3-2
t6-1         t8-1         temp         zonk8
$
```

EXERCISE 2

Historical Data

```
% history
    2 mail
    3 cd /aa/widget/jon/shels
    4 cd /aa/widget/jon/shells
    5 history
    6 cd /aa/jon/shells
    7 cd/ aa/widget/jon/shells
    8 ls -1
    9 mv /aa/widget/donna/camra.c phot.c
   10 pr phot.c ¦ 1 pr
   11 history
%
```

EXERCISE 3

Paragraph Parameters

```
.de NP        \"New Paragraph macro
.sp 3         \" leave 3 blank spaces
.ne 3         \" make sure 3 lines fit on page
.ti +7        \" indent first line 7 spaces
..            \"End of New Paragraph macro
```

Many software programs provide characters that do not appear on the keyboard (i.e., digraphs, symbols, and diacriticals). These character sets must be supported by your printer in order to print on the hard copy.

[1]
[1]

↖
    [Q]
       ↖
         [A]

Zip [A] finger to [1]

```
a aa aaa q qq qqq 1 11 111aq1 1qa aq11
a aa aaa q qq qqq 1 11 111aq1 1qa aq11

111 qq aq1 11q aq1 11qqaa aaqq11 11qa1
111 qq aq1 11q aq1 11qqaa aaqq11 11qa1
```

[Shift] for [!]

Note See Module 4 for more information about the exclamation mark. In this module, let's practice the [!] again.

```
a aa aaa q qq q11 ! !! !1! aq!! !qaq!!
a aa aaa q qq q11 ! !! !1! aq!! !qaq!!

11!! !!11 !1!1 aq1! !1qa aq1!! 1q1!A!!
11!! !!11 !1!1 aq1! !1qa aq1!! 1q1!A!!

Wow! How! Alas! I have 1 cent! Great!!
Wow! How! Alas! I have 1 cent! Great!!

Look out below! Fantastic! Wonderful!!
Look out below! Fantastic! Wonderful!!
```

[2]
[2]

↖
    [W]
       ↖
         [S]

Zip [S] finger to [2]

```
s ss sss w ww www 2 22 222sw2 2ws sw22
s ss sss w ww www 2 22 222sw2 2ws sw22

222 wsw 22wsw2 22ws sw2 2ws ww22 22ws2
222 wsw 22wsw2 22ws sw2 2ws ww22 22ws2
```

UNIX Environment

What is UNIX? UNIX has the same functionality as DOS, and many of its commands are similar. UNIX, however, was written by Bell Laboratories in a computer language called C and and was designed to facilitate uncomplicated computer-to-computer communications.

UNIX allows you to invent your own sets of names for the system commands, change the prompts, replace user interface, and create new commands.

Moving Right Along! Rather than recap much of the information mentioned in the DOS Environment section, let's proceed to some UNIX exercises.

EXERCISES

Type the following exercises *exactly* as they appear.

Note Remember, when you are in a UNIX environment, you are entering data directly into the computer, not into software. The slightest error (a backslash instead of a forward slash, a semicolon instead of a colon) can cause your command to be unclear. So be very careful about spacing and typographical errors. There is no spell checker you can use.

EXERCISE 1

General Input
```
$ ls -1 /bin
-r-xr-xr-r 1 bin 11692 Nov. 15 1:00 ar
-r-xr-xr-r 1 bin 4506  Nov. 15 3:00 as
      <etc...>
-r-xr-xr-r 1 bin 3454  Nov. 15 3:30 cp
      <etc...>
-r-xr-xr-r 1 bin 12304 Nov. 15 4:00 ls
      <etc...>
-r-xr-xr-r 1 bin 23450 Nov. 15 4:30 mv
      <etc...>
-r-xr-xr-r 1 bin 3434  Dec. 15 3:30 uniq
      <etc...>
-r-xr-xr-r 1 bin 12356 Dec. 15 5:30 who
$
```

[Shift] for [@]

```
s  ss  sss  w  ww  www  @  @@  @@@  @sw@@  @ws@@
s  ss  sss  w  ww  www  @  @@  @@@  @sw@@  @ws@@

2  22  22  @  @@  @@  22@@  sw2@@  w@@sw  sw2@@
2  22  22  @  @@  @@  22@@  sw2@@  w@@sw  sw2@@

1  @12  2  @  12  11  @  22  12  @  12.2  1  @  1.2
1  @12  2  @  12  11  @  22  12  @  12.2  1  @  1.2

Invoice 121, 2 pieces @ 12 cents each.
Invoice 121, 2 pieces @ 12 cents each.
```

[3]
[3]
↖
[E]
↖
[D]

Zip [D] finger to [3]

```
d  dd  ddd  e  ee  eee  3  33  333  de3  33ed  d3
d  dd  ddd  e  ee  eee  3  33  333  de3  33ed  d3

de3  3ed  de33  33ed  d33de  33ed3  3ede3  33
de3  3ed  de33  33ed  d33de  33ed3  3ede3  33
```

[Shift] for [#]

```
d  dd  ddd  e  ee  eee  #  ##  ###  de33##  #3ed
d  dd  ddd  e  ee  eee  #  ##  ###  de33##  #3ed

d##e  de3##  #3eed  de3#  dee3#d  de3  3E##d
d##e  de3##  #3eed  de3#  dee3#d  de3  3E##d

#123  #321  #331  #2  #2112  #321  #221  #231
#123  #321  #331  #2  #2112  #321  #221  #231

The numbers were #1, #22, #3, and #23.
The numbers were #1, #22, #3, and #23.
```

```
lastdrive=E
country=001

device=mouse.sys
device=ansi.sys
device=vdisk.sys /E 384

buffers=20
files=30
rem The following commands install mouse and
rem memory, rem drivers, as well as the Marric
disk-rem caching program. The /a switch tells
rem Marric to use expanded memory.
device=c:\mouse.sys
device=c:\net\network.sys
device=c:\bin\himem.sys
device=c:\bin\emm486.exe
device=c:\bin/marric.sys/a
break=on
```

EXERCISE 4

Batch File for Password

```
 1: ECHO OFF
 2: IF "%"==" 555-00-2468" GOTO :access
 3: GOTO :noaccess
 4: :access
 5: CD\ sheryl.dir
 6: set comspec=c:\sheryl.dir\nopath.com
 7: CLS
 8: ECHO ^[[f :moves cursor to home position
 9: PROMPT Welcome to system! $_$p$g
10: You could put the program name here
11: BASICA AUTOBOOT
12: :noaccess
13: ECHO Your Social Security No. isn't valid
14: AUTOEXEC
```

[4]
[4]

[R]

[F]

Zip [F] finger to [4]

```
f ff fff r rr rr 4 44 44 fr4 44rf fr44
f ff fff r rr rr 4 44 44 fr4 44rf fr44

fr4 44r fr44 44rf fr4 4rff ffrr44 44rf
fr4 44r fr44 44rf fr4 4rff ffrr44 44rf
```

[Shift] for [$]

```
f ff fff r rr rrr $ $$ $$$ fr$$ $$rf $
f ff fff r rr rrr $ $$ $$$ fr$$ $$rf $

44$$ $r4$$ fr4$$ $r4f4 $rfr $$rf r44r$
44$$ $r4$$ fr4$$ $r4f4 $rfr $$rf r44r$

I gave $1.22, $2.13, $4.32, and $3.21.
I gave $1.22, $2.13, $4.32, and $3.21.

$3.22, $421.23, $234.12, $44.32, $2.55
$3.22, $421.23, $234.12, $44.32, $2.55
```

[5]
[5]

[R]

[F]

Zip [F] finger to [5]

```
f ff fff r rr rrr 5 55 555 fr5 5tf f55
f ff fff r rr rrr 5 55 555 fr5 5tf f55

fr5 tfg fr5 55rf r55 5tf ffr5 55rf 55r
fr5 tfg fr5 55rf r55 5tf ffr5 55rf 55r
```

[Shift] for [%]

```
fff rrr 555% %%rr 5rrf 5% ft%r fg%% 5%
fff rrr 555% %%rr 5rrf 5% ft%r fg%% 5%

45% ft5 554 f4 234 41g fr5 %%f f4% 44%
45% ft5 554 f4 234 41g fr5 %%f f4% 44%
```

Numbers and Symbols   **46**

Rename a File

```
rename a:oldname newname
rename b:jackson.doc henderson.doc
rename b:part10 chapt10
rename jan95.rpt feb95.rpt
```

Delete a File

```
del c:\test\*.*
del \text\reports\finance.txt
del ..\text\reports\finance.txt
del feb95.rpt
```

EXERCISE 2

```
AUTOEXEC.BAT

path c:\;c:\dos;c:\utility;c:\batch
prompt $p$g
doskey
dosshell

echo off
path
c:\;c:\dos;c:\utility;c:\batch;c:\word;
prompt $p$g
mode 1pt1=com1
mode com1.96,n,8,1,p
set temp=c:\temp
set temp=c:\temp
menu
```

EXERCISE 3

```
CONFIG.SYS

buffers=20
files=30
device=c:\dos\mouse.sys
break=on
break=on
buffers=64
files=20
```

```
25% 45% He scored 11%. 43% 32% 11% %%5
25% 45% He scored 11%. 43% 32% 11% %%5

Sheldon told us 55%, 32%, 12%, and 1%.
Sheldon told us 55%, 32%, 12%, and 1%.
```

Practice

```
1!! 2@@@ 33## saw!! @123 #213 we! see!
1!! 2@@@ 33## saw!! @123 #213 we! see!
$432.23 fr$$ #432 Fred! fast! @2.34 !!
$432.23 fr$$ #432 Fred! fast! @2.34 !!

#321 2 @ 34 dqs!! !@##@! qwe!asd 1s#@3
#321 2 @ 34 dqs!! !@##@! qwe!asd 1s#@3
45% 12% $15.54 Wow! 5@ 25 cents ft%3!!
45% 12% $15.54 Wow! 5@ 25 cents ft%3!!

Wow! Jackie spent $43.14 on groceries.
The bananas were priced: 2 @ 50 cents.
Pay these invoices: #4, #23, and #135.
His percentages were 2%, 24%, and 45%.
```

[6]
[6]

↖

[Y]

↖

[J]

Zip [J] finger to [6]

```
j jj jjj y yy yyy 6 66 666 jy6 6yj j66
j jj jjj y yy yyy 6 66 666 jy6 6yj j66

jy6 6yj jy6 66yj j6 66y jy66 6yjy6 6yj
jy6 6yj jy6 66yj j6 66y jy66 6yjy6 6yj
```

[Shift] for [^]

```
66^^ 6^6^ jy^^ ^yjy6^^Y y hjy 6^^ jy^^
66^^ 6^6^ jy^^ ^yjy6^^Y y hjy 6^^ jy^^

6y^ jhy6^^ ^yjh ^^jj^^ ^yh jy6 jy^ 6yh
6y^ jhy6^^ ^yjh ^^jj^^ ^yh jy6 jy^ 6yh
```

---

it is slightly technical. Once your system has been configured, there is no need to go into the CONFIG.SYS file unless you want to reconfigure it.

AUTOEXEC.BAT After your computer carries out the commands of CONFIG.SYS, it looks for AUTOEXEC.BAT, which is a batch program that defines the characteristics of each peripheral (mouse, printer, modem, etc.) that is connected to your system.

Edlin Edlin is a line-oriented text editor with which you can create and edit ASCII files. It is not a word processor, because its functions are much more limited. Edlin can be used to insert, modify, copy, move, and delete lines of a file. Each line of text will be numbered. (*Note:* Edlin is used in versions released prior to MS-DOS 6.0.)

EXERCISES

Type the following exercises *exactly* as they appear.

Note When you are in a DOS environment, you are entering data directly into the computer, not into software. The slightest error (a backslash instead of a forward slash, a semicolon instead of a colon) can cause your command to be unclear. So, be very careful about spacing and typographical errors. There is no spell checker you can use.

EXERCISE 1

Format a Floppy Disk Caution: Never reformat a hard drive once it has been formatted.

```
format a:
format a:/4
format b:/N:9 /T:80
```

Create a Directory
```
mkdir \property
md \memos
```

Copy a Disk
```
diskcopy a: b:
diskcopy c:\houghtn b:
```

Copy a File
```
copy a:filename.ext b:
copy a:*.* c:\notes
copy a:newfile c:\reports
copy\database\projcts\jones\april\susfigs.asc
copy swallow.typ c:\birds
```

She told me she would úse the ^. When?
She told me she would use the ^. When?
O, Bugs Bunny and Peter Rabbit eat ^^?
O, Bugs Bunny and Peter Rabbit eat ^^?

[7]
[7]
[U]
[J]

[8]
[8]
[I]
[K]

Zip [J] finger to [7]

j jj jjjj u uu uuu 7 77 777 ju7 7uj j7
j jj jjjj u uu uuu 7 77 777 ju7 7uj j7

hu7 77uj ju7 7uj uu7 77u ju77 777 7ju7
hu7 77uj ju7 7uj uu7 77u ju77 777 7ju7

[Shift] for [&]

7 77 777 & && &&& ju7 77u &&u j7& 7&uj
7 77 777 & && &&& ju7 77u &&u j7& 7&uj

77 && 7&&7 ju7 7u jj77 77&& &&jj ju77&
77 && 7&&7 ju7 7u jj77 77&& &&jj ju77&

This & that. His & hers. Yours & mine.
This & that. His & hers. Yours & mine.

This & that & the other thing. 14 & 27
This & that & the other thing. 14 & 27

Zip [K] finger to [8]

k kk kkk i ii iii 8 88 888 88 ii kk i8
k kk kkk i ii iii 8 88 888 88 ii kk i8

ki8 8ik kkii 88ik ki8 888 8ik kki8 8ik
ki8 8ik kkii 88ik ki8 888 8ik kki8 8ik

Numbers and Symbols

Module 13
DOS AND UNIX ENVIRONMENTS _____

DOS Environment

This module will help you recognize DOS and UNIX commands, which are somewhat different from ordinary typing. It will not teach you how to use DOS or UNIX. For such information, please check a DOS or UNIX user manual.

What is DOS? MS-DOS, commonly known as DOS, is the accepted acronym for *D*isk *O*perating *S*ystem. It is a registered trademark of the Microsoft Corporation and is the most widely used operating system for PCs.

A computer needs a manager to administer its operations, just as a company needs a manager to administer its operations. And that is what DOS is. A manager. Quite simply put, DOS manages, controls, and processes the information on the PC.

DOS Prompt The DOS prompt channels your data into a certain disk drive for storage, much like an in box. The prompt, therefore, tells the computer on which disk drive to store the information.

Drives A and B are floppy disk drives. The common hard drive is C, although the hard drive can be subdivided and use the letters D, E, F, etc. The letter followed by a greater than symbol (>) indicates which drive you are using. For example:

A> indicates that you can enter data on floppy drive A.
C> indicates that you can enter data on hard drive C.

Filename Extensions When you name a file, you also should also tell DOS what kind of file it is. This makes for a more organized filing system. Although you can use a dot and any three-letter extension, some common extensions are:

.bat batch files
.com files that contain programs
.doc documents
.exe executable files
.sys files that contain information about your hardware
.txt text files

CONFIG.SYS CONFIG.SYS stands for *config*uring your *sys*tem. This will control how your system will start. CONFIG.SYS is not something you necessarily need to know;

[Shift] for [*]

```
8 88 888 * ** *** kk ii 88 88ik* **ik*
8 88 888 * ** *** kk ii 88 88ik* **ik*

ki8 8** 8I K*K ki88** *iki8* *kKi8 II8
ki8 8** 8I K*K ki88** *iki8* *kKi8 II8

The ** asterisk ** looks like a star.
The ** asterisk ** looks like a star.

* This is the first item in the list.
* This is the second item in the list.
```

[9]
[9]

↖

[0]

↖

[L]

Zip [L] finger to [9]

```
1 11 111 o oo ooo 9 99 999 1o9 99o 119
1 11 111 o oo ooo 9 99 999 1o9 99o 119

19 99o1 1o9o 11o9 99o 999 o119 99o 11o
19 99o1 1o9o 11o9 99o 999 o119 99o 11o
```

[Shift] for [(]

Note

See Module 4 for more information about the opening parenthesis. In this module, let's practice the [(] again.

```
(9(9 1o(( (o1o9((o 11o9 9oo1 (o1o9( 99
(9(9 1o(( (o1o9((o 11o9 9oo1 (o1o9( 99

( is half a parentheses. It is lonely!
( is half a parentheses. It is lonely!

( is searching for its other half.((((
( is searching for its other half.((((
```

Brain Buster #13:   Goof-Proof

Type the following sentences correctly:

Example: The passive voice should rarely be used. = Rarely use the passive voice.

1. Remember to never split an infinitive.
2. A verb should agree with their subject.
3. Proofread carefully to see if words or numbers left out repeated.
4. A writer shouldn't shift their point of view.
5. If any word is inproper at the end of a sentence, a linking verb is.
6. Take the bull by the horn and never mix metaphors.
7. Always pick on the correct idiom.
8. Remember, a preposition isn't a word you should end a sentence with.
9. Last, but not least, avoid clichés like the plague; seek viable alternatives.
10. Avoid trendy locutions that sound flaky.

[0]
[0]

    ↖

      [P]

        ↖

       [;]

Zip [;] finger to [0]

```
; ;; ;;; p pp ppp 0 00 000 ;;p0 0p; p0
; ;; ;;; p pp ppp 0 00 000 ;;p0 0p; p0

00o1 1o0 0p ;;p0 00p; ;;p0 0p;;p 00p;;
00o1 1o0 0p ;;p0 00p; ;;p0 0p;;p 00p;;
```

[Shift] for [)]

Note

See Module 4 for more information about the closing parenthesis. In this module, let's practice the [)] again.

```
0 00 000 ) )) ))) p 00p0);p0)) 00p ;;p
0 00 000 ) )) ))) p 00p0);p0)) 00p ;;p

00 00p;; pp;0)) ))p;p0 00p;; ppOp; ppO
00 00p;; pp;0)) ))p;p0 00p;; ppOp; ppO

) is the other half of the parentheses.
When you type ), ( is no longer lonely.

Barbara (my sister) is standing there.
Barbara (my sister) is standing there.

(1) apple, (2) bananas, and (3) pears.
(1) apple, (2) bananas, and (3) pears.
```

[-]

      [-]

     ↗

   [P]

 ↗

[L]

Zip [l] finger to [-]

Note

See Module 4 for more information on the hyphen. In this module, let's practice the [-] again.

INSTRUCTION	MARK IN MARGIN	MARK ON PROOF	CORRECTED TYPE
GENERAL			
Delete	ℒ	the good word	the word
Delete and close up space	ℒ	the woꞬrd	the word
Insert indicated material	good	the word	the good word
Let it stand	stet	the good word	the good word
Spell out	sp	②words	two words
PARAGRAPHING			
New paragraph	¶	"Where is it?"/"It's on the shelf"	"Where is it?" "It's on the shelf."
Flush paragraph	¶	"Where is it?"/"It's on the shelf"	"Where is it?" "It's on the shelf."
POSITION AND SPACING			
Transpose	tr	the word/good	the good word
Move left	⊏	⊏the word	the word
Move right	⊐	⊐the word	the word
Move down	⊔	⌊the⌋word	the word
Move up	⊓	⌈the⌉word	the word
Align	‖	‖the word the word	the word the word
Straighten line	⹀	the word	the word
Insert space	#	theword	the word
Equalize space	eq #	the good word	the good word
Close up	⌒	the wo rd	the word
en space	⅟N	the word	the word
em space	⅟M	the word	the word
PUNCTUATION			
period	⊙	This is the word	This is the word.
comma	⋀	words words, words	words, words, words
hyphen	⹀	word for word test	word-for-word test
colon	⊙	The following words	The following words
semicolon	⋀	Scan the words/skim the words	Scan the words; skim the words
apostrophe	⌄	Johns words	John's words
double quotation marks	⌄/⌄	the word word	the word "word"
single quotation marks	⌄/⌄	the "good word"	the "good 'word'"
brackets	[/]	He read from the Word in the Bible	He read from the Word [in the Bible]
en dash	⊦	1964 1972	1964–1972
em dash	⊥/M	The dictionary how often it is needed belongs in every home	The dictionary—how often it is needed—belongs in every home
asterisk	⌄	word	word*
dagger	⌄	a word	a word†
double dagger	⌄	words and words	words and words‡
section symbol	§	Book Reviews	§Book Reviews
virgule (slash)	/	either/or	either/or
three ellipses	|⊙|⊙|⊙|	the word	the word
four ellipses	⌒⊙|⊙|⊙|⊙|	the word	the word
STYLE OF TYPE			
uppercase	uc	the word	The Word
lowercase	lc	The Word	the word
small capitals	sc	the word	THE WORD
italic	ital	the entry word	the entry *word*
roman	rom	the entry word	the entry word
boldface	bf	the entry word	the entry **word**
lightface	lf	the entry word	the entry word
superior	²	2²=4	2²=4
inferior	₂	H₂O	H₂O

Just a reminder: The top of the hyphen key has the underscore character. On a computer, however, a character can take up only one space, so you cannot underscore a character using the key. If you need to underscore, use the underscore feature of the software, not the key.

```
sister-in-law, seventy-three, off-line
sister-in-law, seventy-three, off-line
editor-in-chief, twenty-one, 1993-1994
editor-in-chief, twenty-one, 1993-1994

pages 89-146, two-thirds, self-control
pages 89-146, two-thirds, self-control
on-line, part-time job, Marlow-Ferrino
on-line, part-time job, Marlow-Ferrino
```

[=]

    [=]
        ↗
   [[]
   ↗
[;]

Zip [;] finger to [=]

```
; ;; ;;; [ [[ [[[ = == === ;[= =[; ;==
; ;; ;;; [ [[ [[[ = == === ;[= =[; ;==

===[[[[ ;;[[ ;[= ==[; ;;[= =[;;[==[;;=
===[[[[ ;;[[ ;[= ==[; ;;[= =[;;[==[;;=
```

[Shift] for [+]

```
= == === + ++ +++ ;[=++ ++===[[;[[ =+=
= == === + ++ +++ ;[=++ ++===[[;[[ =+=

3 + 5 = 6 Oops! No! 3 + 5 = 8 Better!!
3 + 5 = 6 Oops! No! 3 + 5 = 8 Better!!

1020+1000=2020, 653 + 200 = 853 Right?
1020+1000=2020, 653 + 200 = 853 Right?
```

Practice

```
1 2 3 4 5 6 7 8 9 0 9 8 7 6 5 4 3 2 1
1 2 3 4 5 6 7 8 9 0 9 8 7 6 5 4 3 2 1
```

Feburary 30, 19XX)?

Acme Equipment Company

(SP) 24 Longfellow Rd

(#) Detroit, MI 48256

(#) Dear Sir: [Ladies or Gentlemen:

(#) The maintainance of a good credit rating is vital
to any bussinesman. When you indebtness excedes
your usual credit limit, your in danger of
loosing the good credit standing you've recieved in
the passed.   past

(#) [←—I am very sorry to have to right you this   write
letter but I find that we have aloud your   allowed
indebtness of $1,788.00 to continue much to long.
Unless payment in full is recieved within two
weeks from the date of this letter, you you will
leave us with no alternative but to turn this
matter over to are attorney.   our

Very Truly Yours,

(#)

Miss B. Haven

```
2 4 6 8 10 2 4 6 8 10 2 4 6 8 10  even
2 4 6 8 10 2 4 6 8 10 2 4 6 8 10  even

1 3 5 7 9 1 3 5 7 9 1 3 5 7 9  all odd
1 3 5 7 9 1 3 5 7 9 1 3 5 7 9  all odd
```

He lives at 23 Main Street in Chicago.
Jane spent $125.55 on her school ring.
Michael Wasserman's ZIP code is 10243.
He will leave on September 15 at 2:00.

She had 5 pennies, 3 nickels, 7 dimes,
45 quarters, and 10 silver dollars. Do
you know how much that =? It = $22.15.

Charles is (1) tall, (2) dark, and (3)
handsome. And he got 100% on his test.
On December 1, he paid Gloria $500.00.
John's phone number is (508) 745-3213.

Jack's plane will leave from gate #35.
Invoice #456 (n/30) is due on the 1st.
$1,150.75 represents a savings of 50%.
Pat's picture frame measured 18 by 12.

Progress Check It is time to check your progress once again. Numbers are more difficult than letters, so do not be discouraged if you slowed down slightly.

On October 14, 654 people attended.	7
June 20 marks our 15th anniversary.	14
She was given $5.00 to buy a dress.	21
Kate (my mother) is wearing purple.	28
Did I hear you say it was just 50%?	35

```
1      2      3      4      5      6      7
```

What Exactly is Desktop Publishing? (center)

(DTP) is much more than word processing; its actually creating letterhead, brochures, newsletters, flyers, advertisements, forms, manuals, etc., right from you're computer. You can generate finished professional-quality pages, useing special software that offers typesetting and and graphic capabilities and page make-up functions. The results (be can) generated on a laser printer to be used either as a finished copy or as camera-ready copy for a professional printer.

In days of yore (pre-DTP), after you created a manuscript, you would send it for typesetting, go (thru) rounds of proofreading/revisions, paste the graphics, then send the finished document for printing. If there were changes that had to be implemented at the last minute, you'd have to make the changes, send them back to the typesetter, go through more rounds of proofreading/revisions, repaste the graphics, and then send the document for printing. This process could go on ad nauseam and would often result in major time delays and additional expenses.

When the changes come flying at you fast and furiously, they can be taken care of quickly and painlessly. In a DTP environment, you have control over the entire production process, because you essentially have your own publishing system.

```
She lives at 204 5th Avenue, Salem.        7
Invoice #694 has a balance of $228.       14
Wow! $1,000 is certainly wonderful!       21
Mary was here & there & everywhere.       28
Two gold ** for the one who has it.       35
```

```
1     2     3     4     5     6     7
```

RATE YOURSELF

 7 wpm = fair
14 wpm = good
21 wpm = very good
28 wpm = excellent
35 wpm = superior

Brain Buster #6:   *Letter Perfect*

Each equation contains the initials of words that will complete the expression. Type the complete expression.

Example: 24 = H. in a D. This stands for: 24 = hours in a day

1.   26 = L. of the A.

2.   1,001 = A.N.

3.   12 = S. of the Z.

4.   9 = P. in the S.S.

5.   88 = K. on a P.

6.   13 = S. on the A.F.

7.   32 = D. at which W.F.

8.   90 = D. in a R.A.

9.   8 = S. on a S.S.

10. 4 = Q. in a G.

The following show marked-up versions of Exercises 3, 4, and 5.

Corrections for Exercise 3

]Databases [(center)

Think back for a moment to your good ole school days. *(ital)*
Remember the ordeal of doing a term paper? First, (you'd) *(sp)*
have to find the time to treck off to the library. Then
you would spend hours going through the card catalog,
rummaging through tomes of publications, then copying
(by hand or on a photocopier) all the pertinent
information. Often, you would have to make several
trips in order to a mass all the information you
needed. And did that ever cut into your social plans!
"Wouldn't it be wonderful," you might have thought, "If
all this were available at my fingertips and would
happen by magic. Well, for those of you who can recall
that ordeal, you might have been born too early because
it's not quite magic — but all this is available at
your fingertips.

(indent) Now your needs are a little more sophisticated.
Perhaps you make or influence important decisions for
your company. . . Perhaps you need factual data that
will give you the competitive edge. . . perhaps you
need to get your hands on specific information about
business, finance, sales, marketing, technology,
government, or current events. . . If you do, your
your computer can become a window to data bases for
viewing a broad base of electronic information
services in a matter of minutes. It is not necessary to
spend hours paging through reference books or trade
journals or merely doing without the information. No
matter what kind of information you need — from annual
revenues to annual rainfalls — it is at your
fingertips 24 hours a day, 365 days a year.

Module 6
NUMERIC KEYPAD

Most keyboards have a numeric keypad to the right enabling you to input numerals at high speeds. (Of course, for us "lefties" that takes some getting used to.) If you practice a lot and master the numeric keypad, you might be able to key in 200 digits per minute (dpm). The industry standard is 250 dpm.

The arrangement of the numerals will be the same from one keyboard to another, but the surrounding keys can vary. This is an example of a numeric keypad.

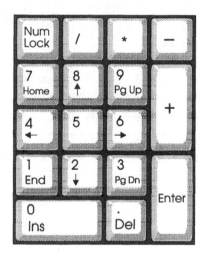

The following is an explanation of the surrounding keys.

[Num Lock] Toggle [Num Lock] on and off. When it is on, you will be using the numbers; when it is off, you will be using the other markings on the keys.

[/] [*] [–] [+] Mathematical functions: divide, multiply, subtract, add.

[Enter] Same as [Enter] on the keyboard.

[Del] Delete data.

[Ins] Toggle between insert mode and overstrike mode.

Feburay 30, 19XX

Acme Equiptment Company
24 Longfellow Rd.
Detroit, MI 48256
Dear Sir:
The maintainance of a good credit rating is vital
to any bussinesman.When you indebtness excedes
your usual credit limit, your in danger of
loosing the good credit standing youve recieved in
the passed.
　　　I am very sorry to have to right you this
letter but I find that we have aloud your
indebtness of $1,788.00 to continue much to long.
UNless payment in full is recieved within two
weeks from the date of this letter, you you will
leave us with no alternative, but to turn this
matter over to are attorney.
　　　　　Very Truly Yours,

　　　　　Miss B. Haven

The home row is [4] [5] [6]. Your index finger will be placed on the 4; the middle finger, on the 5; and the ring finger, on the 6.

Turn on [Num Lock]

Home Row Keys

[4] [5] [6]

```
4  44  444  4444  5  55  555  5555  6  66  666  6666
4  44  444  4444  5  55  555  5555  6  66  666  6666

4  44  555  6666  5  55  666  4444  5  55  555  6666
4  44  555  6666  5  55  666  4444  5  55  555  6666

456  456  4456  4456  4556  4556  4566  4566  456
456  456  4456  4456  4556  4556  4566  4566  456

44  55  66  44  55  66  66  55  44  55  66  44  44  55
44  55  66  44  55  66  66  55  44  55  66  44  44  55
56  45  65  45  56  44  56  64  45  56  64  45  65  44
55  66  65  54  45  56  45  65  45  65  45  55  66  45
```

Top Row Keys

[7]
[7]
↑
[4]

Zip [4] finger to [7]

```
4  44  444  7  77  777  44  77  444  777  47  74  477
4  44  444  7  77  777  44  77  444  777  47  74  477

7  777  774  44  44  747  447  774  447  774  44777
7  777  774  44  44  747  447  774  447  774  44777

45  56  67  76  65  45  47  65  47  75  67  77  74  56
45  56  67  76  65  45  47  65  47  75  67  77  74  56

4567  7654  456  667  675  457  776  765  456  774
4567  7654  456  667  675  457  776  765  456  774
7765  7654  456  777  667  775  774  675  675  745
7765  7654  456  777  667  775  774  675  675  745
```

What Exactly is Desktop Publishing?

DTP is much more than word processing; its actually creating letter head, brochures, flyers, advertisements, forms, manuals, etc., right from you're computer. You can generate finished, professional-quality pages, useing special software that offers typesetting and and graphic capabilities and page make-up functions. The results be can generated on a laser printer to be used either as a finished copy or as camera ready copy for a professional printer.

In days of yore (pre-DTP), after you created a manuscript, you would sent it for typesetting, go thru rounds of proofreading/revisions, paste the graphics, then send the finished document for printing. If there were changes that had to be implemented at last minute, you'd have to make the changes, send them back to the typesetter, go through more rounds of proofreading/revisions, repaste the graphics, and then send the document for printing This process could go on ad nauseam and would often result in major time delays and additional expenses.

When the changes come flying at you fast and furiously, they can be taken care of quick and painlessly. In a DTP environment, you have control over the entire production process, because you essentially have your one publishing system.

[8]
[8]
↑
[5]

Zip [5] finger to [8]

```
5  55  555  8  88  888  55  88  555  888  58  85  588
5  55  555  8  88  888  55  88  555  888  58  85  588

8  888  885  55  55  858  558  885  558  885  55888
8  888  885  55  55  858  558  885  558  885  55888

88  78  65  86  46  87  48  78  56  78  85  48  76  78
88  78  65  86  46  87  48  78  56  78  85  48  76  78

5588  8855  5886  8765  788  5678  8765  6788  78
5588  8855  5886  8765  788  5678  8765  6788  78
5678  8658  7788  8764  488  8678  8756  8766  68
5678  8658  7788  8764  488  8678  8756  8766  68
```

[9]
[9]
↑
[6]

Zip [6] finger to [9]

```
6  66  666  9  99  999  66  99  999  666  69  69  699
6  66  666  9  99  999  66  99  999  666  69  69  699

9  99  998  996  986  9586  695  559  994  458  965
9  99  998  996  986  9586  695  559  994  458  965

98  98  59  58  79  69  69  94  67  86  58  75  69  74
98  98  59  58  79  69  69  94  67  86  58  75  69  74

4685  6998  4896  5879  879  5879  8996  6654  79
4685  6998  4896  5879  879  5879  8996  6654  79
6998  5479  9658  9745  499  9657  7486  6589  96
6998  5479  9658  9745  499  9657  7486  6589  96
```

Bottom Row Keys

[1]
[4]
↓
[1]

Zip [4] finger to [1]

```
4  44  444  1  11  111  41  14  4411  1114  414  114
4  44  444  1  11  111  41  14  4411  1114  414  114
```

Exercises 3, 4, and 5 contain errors. Use proofreaders' marks to identify each error. Then type each exercise correctly. (The marked-up versions are on pages 144–146.)

EXERCISE 3

Databases

Think back for a moment to your good ole school days. Remember the ordeal of doing a term paper? First, you'd have to find the time to treck off to the library. Then you would spend hours going through the card catalog, rummaging through tomes of publications,then copying (by hand or on a photocopier) all the pertinent information. Often, you would have to make several trips in order to a mass all the information you needed. And did that ever cut into your social plans! "Wouldn't it be wonderful," you might have thought, "If all this were available at my fingertips and would happen by magic. Well, for those of you who can recall that ordeal, you might have been born too early because — it's not quite magic — but all this is available at your fingertips.
Now your needs are a little more sophisticated. Prehaps you make or influence important decisions for your company. . . Perhaps you need factual data that will give you the competitive edge. . . perhaps you need to get your hands on specific information about business, finance, sales, marketing, technology, government, or current events. . . If you do, your your computer can become a window to data bases for viewing a broad base of electronic information services in a matter of minutes. It is necessary to spend hours paging through reference books or trade journals or merely doing without the information. No matter what kind of information you need — from annual revenues to annual rainfalls — it is at your fingertips 24 hours a day 365 days a year.

```
147  741  117  741  158  745  587  117  119  81  14
147  741  117  741  158  745  587  117  119  81  14

14  14  87  59  69  54  11  17  91  47  96  64  41  47
14  14  87  59  69  54  11  17  91  47  96  64  41  47

1459  5591  1471  1595  991  1185  6971  4759  91
1459  5591  1471  1595  991  1185  6971  4759  91
5681  9119  1475  5415  199  5874  5511  5698  69
5681  9119  1475  5415  199  5874  5511  5698  69
```

[2]
[5]
↓
[2]

Zip [5] finger to [2]

```
5  55  555  2  22  222  52  25  52  225  552  225  52
5  55  555  2  22  222  52  25  52  225  552  225  52

252  258  852  215  526  254  254  225  85  219  65
252  258  852  215  526  254  254  225  85  219  65

22  55  88  84  52  15  95  65  72  25  96  65  47  95
22  55  88  84  52  15  95  65  72  25  96  65  47  95

1599  6526  625  521  4581  9612  5796  2695  472
1599  6526  625  521  4581  9612  5796  2695  472
6952  2596  148  256  2698  2254  4425  5692  224
6952  2596  148  256  2698  2254  4425  5692  224
```

[3]
[6]
↓
[3]

Zip [6] finger to [3]

```
6  66  666  3  33  333  6  66  3  33  63  36  63  3336
6  66  666  3  33  333  6  66  3  33  63  36  63  3336

369  963  369  553  2596  325  32  3596  3214  477
369  963  369  553  2596  325  32  3596  3214  477

36  36  51  98  92  43  34  82  15  96  35  74  15  63
36  36  51  98  92  43  34  82  15  96  35  74  15  63
```

Private Employment Agencies

Private agencies are excellent sources of job openings. Some agencies specialize in certain types of positions while others may be of a general nature. There is usually a fee involved that may or may not be absorbed by the employers. (Sometimes the fee will be shared.) Although the fee may seem large to you obtaining a position may be well worth the cost.

Professional Association Agencies

Many professions such as nursing, accounting, engineering, word processing, etc., maintain employment agencies for members of their respective professions and for college students entering the profession. Check periodically!

Temporary Agencies

Temporary agencies exist for a wide variety of professions. They offer a variety of experiences, an excellent source of reference, and permanent placement (in some instances).

School Placement Services

High schools, business schools, trade schools, and colleges have well organized placement services. The placement officer will refer you to positions as well as advise you of any problems you may encounter.

```
3583  3591  5153  415  3695  5369  7516  9452  11
3583  3591  5153  415  3695  5369  7516  9452  11
1586  6579  9237  772  2593  3189  6541  1485  58
1586  6579  9237  772  2593  3189  6541  1485  58
```

[0]
[4]
↓
[1]
↓
[0]

Zip [4] finger to [0]

```
4  44  444  1  11  111  0  00  000  014  410  001  40
4  44  444  1  11  111  0  00  000  014  410  001  40

014  410  0258  630  025  890  003  301  108  0117
014  410  0258  630  025  890  003  301  104  3017

01  42  09  93  02  58  94  07  71  01  63  09  92  05
01  42  09  93  02  58  94  07  71  01  63  09  92  05

2058  9503  4712  2593  321  0258  9741  1147  73
2058  9503  4712  2593  321  0258  9741  1147  73
0039  9932  2058  8741  258  5236  9885  2014  65
0039  9932  2058  8741  258  5236  9885  2014  65
```

[.]
[6]
↓
[3]
↓
[.]

Zip [6] finger to [.]

```
6.  3.3  6.6  3.3  3.33  6.66  6.36  63.36  36.63
6.  3.3  6.6  3.3  3.33  6.66  6.36  63.36  36.63

1.1  2.2  3.3  4.4  5.5  6.6  7.7  8.8  9.9  10.00
1.1  2.2  3.3  4.4  5.5  6.6  7.7  8.8  9.9  10.00
```

Phone Numbers
```
316-852-7129
201-783-0288
914-783-3697
516-723-0047

803-641-1867
601-742-3697
919-753-0856
512-752-4173
```

"convenient location" (depending on where you
   live)
"can assume responsibility" (you have to do
   everything?)
"miscellaneous responsibilities" (looking for a
   maid?)
"easy to get along with" (you or ~~them~~ they?)
"must have a driver's license" (with the price
   of gas, they may be looking for a ~~chaufer~~ chauffeur)

Avoid ads that require employees to make a
deposit of of money, to purchase sample goods, etc.
Such advertisements may merely be ploys to sell
goods. Most ads will ask that you submit a resume
or will list a number you should call. If a post
office box is given, the prospective employer does
not want people dropping in. The resume gives the
employer the opportunity to review your
qualifications and background and make ~~and make~~ a
selection.

Public Employment Agencies
   In 1933 the United States Employment Services
was established, and today State Employment
Agencies are located throughout the United States
in convenient locations. You will never have to pay
for this service since ~~as~~ the agency is subsidized
through taxes.

Note

The decimal points should align.

```
$4,123.12
 9,232.47
   902.17
 7,418.92

   712.365
    89.257
   123.009
     7.360
```

Progress Check

It is time to check your progress. At this point you certainly will *not* be typing 200 dpm. However, with practice, your speed will increase.

1 4 8 5	26	31	48	852	114	79	635	001		7
3 0 2 8	52	19	93	295	159	37	357	587		14

1	2	3	4	5	6	7

345	679	901	263	321	147	741	123	121	7
387	741	369	002	258	147	789	963	256	14
203	682	005	510	119	663	228	841	123	21
306	650	258	951	147	474	336	920	147	28
369	521	147	985	220	036	541	752	210	35

1	2	3	4	5	6	7

EXERCISE 2

POUNDING THE PAVEMENT

Once you have acquired the necessary skills and have zeroed in on a profession or trade, finding an appropriate placement is your next step. If you cannot rely on other people to get you a job—you must "sell yourself." Many people complain that there are no jobs out there. Remember, no one will come knocking at your door; it is you who must take the initiative. Inform friends, relatives, and former employers of your quest, and immediately follow up all leads. Send resumes to local companies in which you are interested, check the want ads, register with employment agencies, contact your school placement service, and most important of all, PERSEVERE!

Want Ads

Check regularly the want ads of your local newspaper to familiarize yourself with the types of jobs that are available and the salaries connected with them. Remember, however, that only 20% of the available jobs are listed in the want ads, and many may have already been filled.

Be aware of the language used in these want ads and what they really mean.

"fee paid" (by whom?)
"excellent benefits" (low pay?)

```
22  14  78  52  36  95  02  02  22  30  25  55        7
36  02  10  15  36  95  20  14  07  52  02  64       14
52  21  47  96  32  58  56  90  01  13  14  22       21
32  02  58  79  14  21  12  23  36  58  74  40       28
39  99  55  11  47  12  56  30  09  58  74  11       35

 1       2       3       4       5       6       7
```

Brain Buster #7: *Beastasaurus Rex*

Type the "animal" expressions used for the following.

Example: nag one's mate = henpeck

1. people who stay up late
2. warring
3. pretend to be asleep
4. stubborn
5. not too young
6. have an honest discussion
7. test case
8. final annoyance that pushes one to the limit
9. gluttonous
10. generous supplier

The following exercises have been proofread and edited. Type each one carefully and correctly.

DRESSING FOR BUSINESS

Have you ever walked into an office and have been greeted by a secretary wearing a halter or flimsy blouse and miniskirt? Just think of the image that conjures up. The image is a negative one, reflecting poorly on the secretary and the office. This kind of attire might be appropriate for a secretary working in a hotel in Acapulco, but is it not appropriate for a secretary working in a conventional office. Be aware of separating your professional wardrobe and your leisure wardrobe. What you wear makes a statement about your attitudes, your goals, your moods, and your feelings. If you want to get ahead in the business world, dress appropriately.

Dress standards vary in different parts of the country. For example, in Calif. and Florida, warm weather climates, people tend to dress more simply and casually than their counter parts in New York and boston, where dress tends to be savvy, accessorized and chic. In Washington, DC, the center of politics, and in the midwest, dress tends to be more understated. Also, some industries, such as banking, call for conservative clothing. Observe those in your organization whom you admire and whose jobs you would like to have, and pattern your habits after those people.

Module 7
WORDS, WORDS, WORDS!

The following exercises incorporate a variety of typewriting skills. Type each exercise *exactly* as it appears.

User Manual

Refer to your User Manual for the following:

- Left Justify
- Center Justify
- Right Justify
- Accents and Diacritical Marks

EXERCISE 1

Letter Combinations

Vowels and Diphthongs

ai

```
chains daily praise sailing tailgate Saint
unfailing trail mailbags Haiti grains jail
quaint nailbrush maintenance paid rainbows
raise praiseworthy prairie mainframe faint
gainsay haircut assail aisle caisson aioli
```

ea

```
ear each teachers teaches beach breach leach
beads leader least reach reached reads ready
sea seas meals seals real steam earnest zeal
gear early earnings earth earthly eaves bear
peaceful beaches dead lead earliest earldoms
```

ei

```
heir rein receive conceit either neither
surveillance freight seize leisure reign
height weight neighborhood their receipt
ceiling sleigh counterfeit neigh foreign
perceive deign skein feigned deity ceiba
forfeited seizure seismic meiosis either
```

Rail

Although no single mode of transportation will be able to meet the full range of transportation needs, our rail rail system has always been, and continued to be one of the hall marks of our nations transportation infrastructure.

RAIL

Although no single mode of transportation will be able to meet the full range of transportation needs, our rail system has always been, and continues to be, one of the hallmarks of our nation's transportation infrastructure.

Timed Typing

When you proofread, you are trying to find all the	10
mistakes. Are there any letters in a word omitted?	20
Are there extra letters in a word? Are any letters	30
transposed? Are words properly capitalized? Is the	40
punctuation correct? Are words transposed? Are all	50
the quotation marks both opened and closed? Is the	60
formatting correct? Did you double-check spellings	70
of names? Are the dates correct? Have you used the	80
spell checker in your software? Did you verify the	90
continuity of numbering schemes, such as pages and	100
numeric listings? Have you paid close attention to	110
homonyms? Remember....quality control is your job.	120

1   2   3   4   5   6   7   8   9   10

ia

piano pianist biased hiatus Iberian Miami
phobias riata Siamese diabolic MIA liable
liaisons giants fiasco dialogues diamonds
CIA utilitarian editorial material sialic
bacteria negotiable financially essential
ecclesiastical Niagara diastasis hysteria

ie

ancient glacier quiet proficient species
lieu thief view lien piety sienna shield
relief wield lief chief friend frontiers
client belief relieve handkerchief fiend
yield field achieve interview sufficient
hygienic fiercely fiendish diesel diesis

oi

oil choice diploid poignant point toilet
soiree roister roil moisturizer toilsome
loitered loincloth adjoining hoity-toity
doily coin coinage coincide coincidental
boilerplate boisterous pointless jointed

ou

oust couch boundary count thought fought
louder pounce country county counterfeit
grouch our yours mountain outfield route
tournament tourism southern poultry sour
roughness quotation Louis boulevard four
fourth doubles grounded joyous household

EXERCISE 2

Consonants

ch

cheer each watch hatch check chore chain
chicken teach teacher grouch pouch peach
peachy much latch chews chairperson inch
cinches rich richer richest chose choose
chronic clutch brochure church bronchial
cherished enchantment Christian achieves

Module 12
PROOFREADING AND EDITING _____

```
Eye here ewe.
Eye sea ewe.
Eye no ewe.
```

Each document should be checked carefully for formatting, styling, English usage, word repetition, omissions, spacing, transpositions, hyphenations, names and addresses, numbers, spelling, and the general sense of the text.

Computers have greatly simplified the process of proofreading and editing, but they do not take the place of the human eye. For example, many software programs have built-in spelling checkers, but a spelling checker cannot differentiate between homonyms (*eye, I; here, hear; ewe, you;* or *sea, see*) and will not detect a word that is used incorrectly. Some software programs have a built-in thesaurus and/or grammar checker, but again, you should read, read, and reread!

User Manual

Refer to your User Manual for the following:

- Spelling Checker
- Thesaurus
- Grammar Checker

Helpful Hints

- Use the proofreading and editing features of your software as a backup, *not* as the only means of detecting errors and inconsistencies.
- If you are preparing a draft that might need correction or editing, you should double-space the copy.

Proofreaders' Marks

A complete chart of standard proofreaders' marks appears on page 147.

The following paragraph appears with proofreaders' marks and as corrected copy.

ck

check sickness thick thicker thickest pickle
quick mackerel chuck back duckweed bickering
acknowledgment pack package o'clock rocketry
Rocky Rockies tackle tacky tackiness cracker
crackling wacky checking hackneys greenstick
fickle dicker duck reckless poppycock ruckus

fl

flame flagitious muffled flamboyant flavor
flan inflation flaw flashlight flat-footed
Flemish float fluid flowers deflower flood
fluctuated fluoridate fluster fluorocarbon
fledglings inflexible inflammable inflated
affliction affluence influenced conflation

ght

right bright fight flight might mightier
sought ought height unsightly thoughtful
thoughtless sightless righteous frighten
tightrope drought draught lights freight
heightened weight insight frighten tight

nd

end and founds stand stranded expandable
fund grind ground lend sender underscore
handiest endlessly condolences standards
recommend pretend land landed contending
landlord London abound compound handling
indent plundered panda expand expandable

nt

current event continual meant continents
hint printouts spent pantomime gentleman
mentally intelligently intensive antenna
antagonist entered banter central dental
gentlemen latent pent sentence ventilate
tentatively faintly quaintly paint Saint

Brain Buster #12: *Hyperboles, Metaphors, and Clichés*

Type these figures of speech that are either trite or grossly exaggerated.

Example: unreal = phony as a $3 bill.

1. raining heavily
2. starving
3. gluttony
4. very elderly
5. extremely busy
6. extremely gabby
7. irate
8. speeding
9. familiarity
10. avid reader

ph

photo photograph photographer photography physicians physiological physical physics physique phonetic unphotogenic phonograph phase pharmacy phalanx graph sophisticate phi sophomore aphid aphrodisiac Aphrodite ophthalmological hermaphrodite phenomenon

qu

quota quite quit quiet equals equated aqua equality equip equity aqua quote quotation quarry quarreled qualify quartz quadrupled unqualified unique quarter quarterly Queen quest quaked earthquake quickening banquet quick quicker quickest acquaint aquamarine

sh

should wish mash shovel show showroom shell shopping shimmer pushover publishing relish mushroom leash kinship Washington refreshes shrine devilish shellac shame shield upshot foreshadows rushing inshore bashful ashamed wishy-washy sheltered sheathe shebang sharp

st

stop stay steer yeast first last least longest student stubborn thirsty worst straight strike statistical persistent moist industrial history honest feasts forecast strays dusty customers stormy bookstore astronaut opportunist latest osteopath stereotype stethoscope stern

str-

straight stretchers stricken strew stress strangely street structures strove strung strychnine strudel struggle strong stroll strophe stroke stripling stringent string

EXERCISE 6

Works Consulted • top-bound

Works Consulted

"Aristotle." *Webster's New Biographical Dictionary.* Springfield, Mass.: Merriam-Webster, Inc., 1983.

Brushaw, Charles T., Gerald J. Alred, and Walter E. Oliu. *Handbook of Technical Writing.* 2d ed. New York: St. Martin's Press, 1982.

Chambers, Robert. *Cyclopaedia of English Literature.* 2 vols. New York: World Publishing House, 1987.

Dyer, Richard, "The New View at Tanglewood." *Boston Globe,* June 10, 1994, p. 49.

Effective Business Communication. Boston: Houghton Mifflin Company, 1992.

Foner, Eric, and John A. Garraty, eds. *The Reader's Companion to American History.* Boston: Houghton Mifflin Company, 1991.

Hart, James D. *The Oxford Companion to American Literature.* 5th ed. New York: Oxford University Press, 1983.

Smiley, Xan. "Misunderstanding Africa." *Atlantic,* September 1982, pp. 70—79.

Velasquez, Joyce A. "The Format of Formal Reports." Report prepared for the Southern Engineering Company. Johnson City, Miss. May 29, 1985.

---

th	the this that those these though thought

| | the this that those these though thought
thank throng they theory thesis southern
northern with without health wealth thin
thick therefore thunder therapist worthy
width youthfully theater thicket thinner
throat menthol methodical plethora three |

th
the this that those these though thought
thank throng they theory thesis southern
northern with without health wealth thin
thick therefore thunder therapist worthy
width youthfully theater thicket thinner
throat menthol methodical plethora three

tr
tree trace truth true truism trout trade
truly untrue trust trial trail ventricle
trivial travels traitor trait triangular
sentry intrepid intrastate intrude truck
putrid tributary entreaty country putrid
trinket atrophied transfusion trichnosis

EXERCISE 3

Complete the Word

Type each word and insert the missing *a* and/or *o*.

v_lume	th_nk	kn_w	s_n
c_nn_t	re_ch	s_ci_l	at_p
f_ll_w	h_ppy	_bout	br__d

Type each word and insert the missing *i* and/or *e*.

beh_nd	d_ta_l	_nch	r_cent
fa_nt	caus_	l_ed	_rase
lin_s	fr__nd	n__ghbor	s_nd

EXERCISE 4

Three-, Four-, and Five-Letter Words

Three-Letter Words
owl vow cab its ask yet oar map far hag axe
lip and but his was met sat fit net lot due
fib kit rat fan got gin quo yes our gym its
ass get inn tax box wow put yap keg lob cab

Words, Words, Words!

Works Cited   • left-bound

Works Cited

1"   1.   Jennie Mason, *Introduction to Word Processing* (Indianapolis: Bobbs-   1"
Merrill, 1981), p. 55.

2.   John E. Warriner and Francis Griffith, *English Grammar and Composition* (New York: Harcourt Brace Jovanovich, 1977), p. 208.

3.   Ruth I. Anderson et al., *The Administrative Secretary: Resource* (New York: McGraw-Hill, 1970), p. 357.

4.   Simone de Beauvoir, *The Second Sex*, trans. and ed. H.M. Parshley (New York: Alfred A Knopf, 1953), p. 600.

5.   Alfred H. Markwardt, *American English*, ed. J.L. Dillard (New York: Oxford University Press, 1980), p. 94.

6.   Martha L. Manheimer, *Style Manual: A Guide for the Preparation of Reports and Dissertations*, Books in Library and Information Science, vol. 5 (New York: Marcel Dekker, 1973), p. 14.

7.   Charles T. Brushaw, Gerald J. Alred, and Walter E. Oliu, *Handbook of Technical Writing*, 2d ed. (New York: St. Martin's Press, 1982), pp. 182–184.

8.   National Micrographics Association, *An Introduction to Micrographics*, rev. ed. (Silver Spring, Md.: National Micrographics Association, 1980), p. 42.

9.   *The World Almanac and Book of Facts* (New York: Newspaper Enterprises Association, Inc., 1985), p. 310.

10.   *Rules for Alphabetical Filing as Standardized by ARMA* (Prairie Village, Kans.: Association of Records Managers and Administrators, 1981), p. 14.

11.   Peggy F. Bradbury, ed., *Transcriber's Guide to Medical Terminology* (New Hyde Park, N.Y.: Medical Examination Publishing Co., 1973), p. 446.

12.   Kemp Malone, "The Phonemes of Current English," *Studies for William A. Read*, ed. Nathaniel M. Caffee and Thomas A. Kirby (Baton Rouge: Louisiana State University Press, 1940), p. 133–165.

13.   Robert Chambers, *Cyclopaedia of English Literature*, 2 vols. (New York: World Publishing House, 1875), vol. I, p. 45.

Four-Letter Words	kept envy join pots next zone quit sell pale gave oxen fuel isle calf maid zany quit sell them send were next mine your ours them want vest quit many oust yarn belt rest over hate
Five-Letter Words	audit panel poets title quite unite haven given woven merit chair ivory yearn liver zoned world eight forth laugh knife forty petty truly earns quest about doubt could

EXERCISE 5

Separate Hands

Left Hand Only	war bet far axe fare beat gave rave freed saw few car bar were cave ears rest tease
Right Hand Only	him pop pin hum jump punk plum jolly knoll lip pun mop noun moon hymn onion limp milk

EXERCISE 6

Seeing Double

Double Letters	see off doll feel been putt huff happy fully all ill took noon buzz room look marry nippy inn aah mitt ooze feet ally jazz weeds mommy egg odd adds errs teem bull till funny savvy freedom loosely dapper little dabbled manner beetle Balaam Ossian pizza sniffle storeroom heel foolish aardvarks assistance bookkeeper coolant engrossing letter pannier toothbrush

EXERCISE 7

Popular Phrases

Common Phrases	thank you/ as soon as/ we shall be happy/ if you have/ have you/ of the/ with us/ from you/ you should/ we are/ after which/ if you can/ this is/ that was/ if you have/ of course/ I hope

---

Words, Words, Words!

EXERCISE 4

Body of Report
- left-bound
- two columns
- left justify
- footnote with superscript

Purpose

This study documents the benefits and costs of potential U.S. Coast Guard Vessel Traffic Services (VTS) in selected U.S. deep draft ports on the Atlantic, Gulf, and Pacific coasts. The U.S. Department of Transportation, Research, and Special Programs Administration (RSPA), Volpe National Transportation Systems Center (VNTSC) conducted the study for the U.S. Coast Guard, Office of Navigation Safety and Waterway Services, Special Projects Staff. The study started in February 1990 as a Coast Guard initiative, prior to the passage of the "The Oil Pollution Act of 1990" (Public Law 101-380). This initiative satisfies the requirements of the Act.

Background

The concept of VTS has gained international acceptance by govern-ments and maritime industries, as a means of advancing safety in rapidly expanding ports and waterways. Vessel Traffic Services work through position and situation advisory communica-tions with vessels navigating the waterways. VTS communications are advisory in nature, providing timely and accurate information to the mariner, thus enhancing the potential for avoiding vessel casualties. VTS do not exercise direct control by ordering specific course directions or speeds to maneuver around hazards. "While the Vessel Control Center (VTC) will have the authority to direct the movement of a vessel in a dangerous situation, a master remains responsible for the safe and prudent maneuvering of the vessel at all times."[1]

Several spills following within three months of the Prince William Sound incident of March 1989 (i.e., one in the coastal waters of Rhode Island, one in the Delaware River, and one in the Houston Ship Channel) drew intense congressional interest and resulted in the passage of "The Oil Pollution Act of 1990" (Public Law 101-380) on August 18, 1990. The Act requires the "Secretary to conduct a study . . . to determine and prioritize the U.S. ports and channels that are in need of new, expanded, or improved vessel traffic service systems. . . ." The Act further requires that the results of the study be submitted to Congress not later than one year after enactment of the Act.

Several studies have been performed prior to this study:

1. The USCG Study Report-Vessel Traffic Systems Analysis of Port Needs (August 1973)
2. The BMC Hong Kong VTS Study,

---

[1] Federal Register, Vol. 55, No. 166, August 27, 1990, Rules and Regulations, pg. 34909

Letter Phrases   as you know/ this will confirm/ on behalf of/
as soon as possible/ enclosed you will find/
we would appreciate/ our records show that/
please take this opportunity/ in response to/
self-addressed, stamped envelope

Salutations   Dear Sir or Madam:/ Ladies and Gentlemen:/
Dear Mr. Anthony:/ Dear Mrs. McGulloch:/
To Whom This May Concern:/ To the Staff:

Complimentary   Very truly yours,/ Yours truly,/ Sincerely,/
Closings   Sincerely yours,/ Respectfully yours,/ Yours
respectfully,/ Cordially,/ Best wishes,

EXERCISE 8

Foreign Expressions

Use accent marks where appropriate.

à la mode/ avant-garde/ bona fide/ bon appétit/
carte blanche/ señora/ maitre d'hôtel/ per
diem/ modus operandi/ résumé/ ex post facto/
prima facie/ garçon/ santé/ ad hoc/ carpe diem

EXERCISE 9

Building a Sentence

User Manual
Left Justify   Always
Always be
Always be sure
Always be sure to
Always be sure to keep
Always be sure to keep your
Always be sure to keep your eyes
Always be sure to keep your eyes on
Always be sure to keep your eyes on the
Always be sure to keep your eyes on the copy!

---

background with dark printing. The following are some basic colors and the emotions or responses they invoke.

COLOR	EMOTION/RESPONSE
Pink	Gets a message across and subdues anger. (Why do you think they call it a "pink slip"?)
Yellow	Optimistic and cheery—will get an audience's attention.
Dark Blue	Puts everyone in a soothing and tranquil mood.
Pale Blue	Good in the summer because it can make people feel the room is actually 3—4 degrees cooler than it actually is.
Red	Demands attention and makes people alert.
Green	Shows speed.

Design Criteria

When you are preparing any visual, keep in mind visibility, clarity, and simplicity. All visuals should have a uniform look. Use uppercase and lowercase for the text; it will be easier to read than all capital letters. The headings can be in all capital letters.

2

Center Justify

```
                        It's
                   It's important
                  It's important to
                 It's important to be
              It's important to be computer
          It's important to be computer literate
        It's important to be computer literate now.
```

Right Justify

```
                                                    Be
                                               Be sure
                                            Be sure to
                                      Be sure to check
                                Be sure to check every
                        Be sure to check every homonym
              Be sure to check every homonym carefully.
```

EXERCISE 10

Homonyms and Commonly Confused Words

Type the sentences below and include the missing word from the choices to the left. The correct answers appear at the end of this module.

to, two, too   1. The _____ attorneys had _____ many decisions _____ make.

a lot, allot   2. _____ of people do not _____ their time wisely.

capital, capitol   3. The _____ is located in Boston, the _____ of Massachusetts.

their, they're,   4. _____ going to establish _____ new
there   business over _____ if permission is granted.

correspondence,   5. The three _____ sent their
correspondents   _____ via air mail, but it did not arrive for three days.

Body of Report
- top-bound
- double-spaced
- page numbers should be centered at the bottom of the page

GENERAL PRINCIPLES FOR PREPARING VISUALS

The purpose of a visual is to reinforce and clarify an idea; it should not contain any-one's verbatim presentation. Equate a slide or viewgraph with an article in a magazine. The picture in a magazine is the highlight that is supported by the text. Slides and viewgraphs should be the highlights to reinforce and drive home the speaker's main points. Visuals are effectively used to

- open a presentation
- channel thinking
- emphasize key points
- represent numerical or financial information
- show comparisons
- simplify a process
- explain a new concept

Do not plan too many visuals for a single presentation. Only the high points need to be illustrated, not every thought.

Understanding the Effects of Color

Color has been shown to have an emotional appeal to which people respond. It is recommended that slides be prepared on a dark background with lighter printing and that viewgraphs be prepared on a lightly tinted

1

---

personnel, personal

6. The _____ department has access to all the company's records. Some are rather _____.

chose, choose

7. I _____ the red dress; you should _____ the blue one.

who's, whose

8. _____ going to take _____ place in the race tomorrow?

its, it's

9. _____ the right time for the corporation to make _____ decision.

principal, principle

10. The _____ is a woman of very high _____s.

stationery, stationary

11. The _____ tables could not be removed for the _____ to be displayed.

quite, quiet

12. They were _____ at home in the _____ neighborhood.

except, accept

13. I will _____ the offer, _____ for the deadline. We need more time.

past, passed

14. In the _____, I _____ your house on the way from work.

than, then

15. The brown house costs more _____ the blue; _____ comes the brown.

already, all ready

16. I _____ told you that we will be _____ no later than nine.

all together, altogether

17. The family was _____ for the reading of the will, but no one was _____ pleased with its contents.

Words, Words, Words!   **69**

LIST OF FIGURES

all right, alright 18. Will it be _____ to make the delivery tomorrow?

sight, site 19. The _____ of the new building is a scenic _____.

later, latter 20. Of the two books, the _____ is the _____ edition.

advise, advice 21. I _____ you not to give out free _____.

no, know 22. I _____ there is _____ chance that he is correct.

altar, alter 23. After the bride and groom meet at the _____ it will be a little too late to _____ their relationship.

assistance, assistants 24. His three _____ were of great _____ during his long illness.

beside, besides 25. _____ the chair, the basket is _____ the desk.

board, bored 26. The _____ of Directors was _____ with the agenda.

done, dun 27. Please do not _____ me any further. As soon as the audit is _____ I will remit my check.

illicit, elicit 28. The con man was trying to _____ money for his _____ project.

farther, further 29. I am _____ from home than I expected, but I don't expect any _____ delays.

Words, Words, Words!

formally, formerly

30. They were all dressed _____ for the dance and met all those students who were _____ classmates.

maybe, may be

31. I _____ out of town tomorrow. So _____ you should call before you stop by.

trial, trail

32. The _____ proved that the defendant left a _____ a mile long.

raise, raze

33. The company was willing to _____ the building but would not _____ salaries.

ad, add

34. Please _____ the _____ to your scrapbook.

compliment, complement

35. A full _____ of colors arrived, and I must _____ you on your efforts in bringing it about.

Answers

1. two, too, to
2. A lot, allot
3. capitol, capital
4. They're, their, there
5. correspondents, correspondence
6. personnel, personal
7. chose, choose
8. Who's, whose
9. It's, its
10. principal, principle
11. stationary, stationery
12. quite, quiet
13. accept, except
14. past, passed
15. than, then
16. already, all ready
17. all together, altogether
18. all right (*alright* isn't a word)
19. site, sight
20. latter, later
21. advise, advice
22. know, no
23. altar, alter
24. assistants, assistance
25. Besides, beside
26. Board, bored
27. dun, done
28. elicit, illicit
29. farther, further
30. formally, formerly
31. may be, maybe
32. trial, trail
33. raze, raise
34. add, ad
35. complement, compliment

EXERCISE 2

Table of
Contents from
Technical Report

- left-bound
- set tab for leaders and right justify

Brain Buster #8:   *Foodaholic*

Type the "food" expressions used for the following.

Example: cramped = packed in like sardines

1. crazy
2. stuck
3. lousy car
4. flatter
5. very tall and very slim
6. hunky-dory
7. poking around
8. easy
9. that's the way it is
10. redhead

EXERCISE 1

Cover Page
- top- and bottom-centered
- center justify

AN EXPERIMENTAL STUDY TO DETERMINE THE
EFFECT OF THE SPELLING TEST ON
THE ABILITY OF STUDENTS TO SPELL

Presented to
the Faculty of the
Department of Business Education
and Office Systems Administration
Montclair State College

by
Sheryl Lorenz
B.S., Saint Thomas Aquinas College

December 19XX

Module 8
PREFIXES AND SUFFIXES _____

Prefixes

Note

Most prefixes are joined to a root word without a hyphen unless the second element begins with a capital letter, e.g., *anti-American*. An exception is the prefix *self-*, which is joined to the second element with a hyphen in all but a few instances, e.g., *selfdom, selfhood*. The prefix *re-* is normally joined to a root word without a hyphen unless a distinction must be made between words having more than one meaning, e.g., *recreation*, "sport, play," and *re-creation*, "a new creation."

Type each of the following words.

ante-

antebellum antecede antechamber antedate
antediluvian antefix antemeridian antemortem
antenatal antepenultimate anterior anteroom

anti-

anti-American antiaircraft antibody anticlimactic
antidote antifreeze antigen antigravity antipasto
antipathy antipersonnel antipoverty antisocial
antithesis antitoxin antiviral antiwar

bi-

biannual biathlon biaxial bicarbonate bicentenary
bicentennial bicycle biennial bifocals biform
bigamist bilateral bilingual bimonthly binary
binocular binomial bisect bisexual biweekly

bio-

biochemical biochemistry biodegradable
biodynamics biogenesis biographer biography
biology biomass biomedical bionics biophysics

circum-

circumcise circumduction circumference circumflex
circumlocution circumlunar circumnavigate
circumpolar circumscribe circumscription
circumsolar circumspect circumstantial circumvent

Styling for Technical Papers or Government Reports

Technical papers and government reports adhere to the guidelines of formal reports; however, they are generally quite rigid in format. There is often a unique numbering scheme that identifies each heading and subdivision.

Numbering Headings and Subdivisions

```
1.0 MAIN HEADING

    1.1 FIRST SUBDIVISION
    1.2 SECOND SUBDIVISION

        1.2.1 Next Level Subdivision
        1.2.2 Next Level Subdivision

            1.2.2.1 Next Level Subdivision
            1.2.2.2 Next Level Subdivision
```

Contents of Technical Papers or Government Reports

Reports of this nature will contain any or all of the following: a cover, title page, preface, table of contents (including a list or lists of figures and tables), executive summary, list of acronyms, appendixes, references, and index.

The following exercises are from a variety of reports and manuscripts. Type each one and refer to the styling mentioned earlier in this Module.

Note

If you are using a font other than Courier 12, your report will not match this one line for line.

com-	comfort commence comment commerce commingle commissioner commit common commune communicate communism compare comparison compassion compatible compel complect complete complex complicate complicity compliment complimentary component compose compound comprehend comprehensible comprehension compress compulsive
con-	concern concert conclude concrete condominium conduce conduct confer conference confide confident confine confinement confiscate conflict conflicting congeal conjugate conjunct consider consideration console consolidate construct converge conversation converse convict convince
dis-	disappoint disarm disarrange disband discharge discipline discuss disfavor disfranchise dishonor disinherit disinterested dislocate disloyal dismember dismiss disorganize disperse dispose disposition dispute disrespectful disrobe
em-	embankment embark embarrass embathe embed embellish embezzle embitter embodiment embody embryo empanada empathy emperor employ employee
en-	enable enact enamor encapsulate enchant enclosure encompass encyclical encyclopedia endanger endorsement endow energy engagement engrave enhance enlist enrage enroll entangle enthuse enthusiastic envelope envoy enwind enwrap
for-	forbearance forever forfeit forget forgiveness forgo forjudge forlorn formerly formidable forsake forsooth forswear forward forwarn

Quotations	1. If a quotation is contained within the paragraph, place quotation marks around the quoted material. 2. If a quotation appears as a separate block, it can be used without quotation marks. The quoted material should be indented from the left and right margins and should be single-spaced.
Pagination	The first page of a report (or chapter of a report) is usually not numbered, although it is considered to be page 1. Your software can suppress the number on the first page.
Footnotes and Endnotes or Works Cited	Whenever you are citing work from another source (whether it is a fact, an opinion, or a quote), you must reference the source. Footnotes, which are no longer popular, are included at the bottom of the page on which the text is cited. Endnotes, also referred to as *Works Cited*, are listed at the end of the manuscript. All cited entries should be numbered and appear in numerical order.
Bibliographies or Works Consulted	Bibliographies are commonly referred to as *Works Consulted*. This would include any material that was used as a reference. All entries should be in alphabetical order by the author's last name.

Timed Typing

```
Itineraries help a traveler keep track of all his/    10
her appointments. When making travel arrangements,    20
it would be helpful to contact a travel agent. The    30
travel agent can help plan the itinerary, make the    40
arrangements, and supply necessary information. If    50
you don't know of a travel agent, contact American    60
Society of Travel Agents. Its address is 666 Fifth    70
Avenue, 12th Floor, New York, NY 10103. The travel    80
agent will need information such as name, dates of    90
departure and arrival, mode of transportation, and   100
all the details of your trip. If you have a hectic   110
schedule, why not let someone else do the legwork!   120

  1     2     3     4     5     6     7     8     9    10
```

fore-	forearm forecast foredeck foredoom forego foregoing forehand forehead foreknowing foreleg foreman foremost forenamed forenoon foreordain foreperson forerunner foresight forestall foretell forewarn forewoman foreword
hyper-	hyperacid hyperactive hyperbole hyperbolic hyperboloid Hyperborean hypercharge hypercorrect hypercritical hyperinflation hypermarket hypermedia hypermetric hyperon hyperopia hypersensitive hypersonic hypertension hyperthyroid hypertonic hyperventilation
hypo-	hypoacidic hypoallergenic hypocenter hypochondria hypocrisy hypocritical hypodermic hypodermis hypogene hypoglycemia hyposensitive hypostasis hypothalamus hypothermia hypothesis hypothesize hypothetical hypothyroidism hypoventilation
Inter-	interactive interbank intercede interchange intercity intercollegiate intercontinental interdepartmental interfaith intergalactic interlace interlibrary interlock intermingle intermission intermural internalize international internist interoffice interplantetary interpret interrelated interrogate intersect intersection
intra-	intracellular intracoastal intradermal intragalactic intramolecular intramural intramuscular intraocular intrapersonal intraspecific intrastate intravascular
intro-	introduce introduction introductory introjection introspection introspective introversion

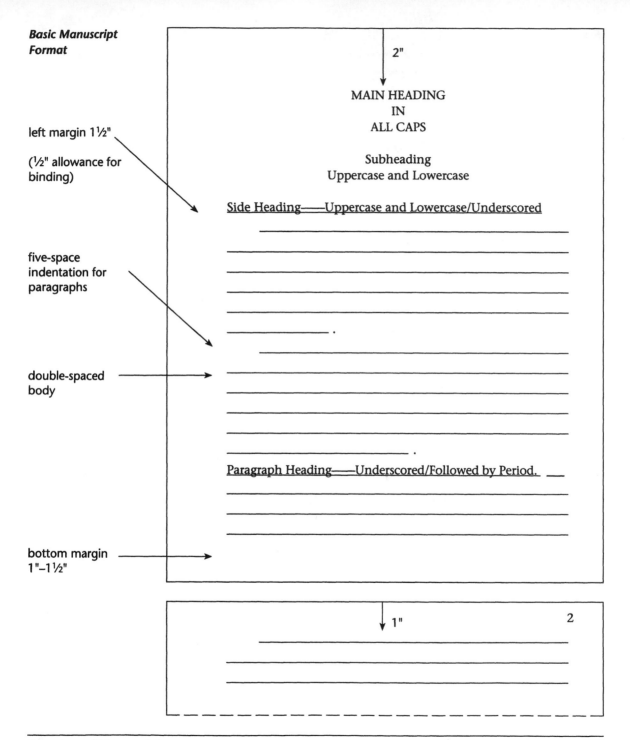

Basic Manuscript Format

2"

MAIN HEADING
IN
ALL CAPS

Subheading
Uppercase and Lowercase

left margin 1½"

(½" allowance for binding)

<u>Side Heading——Uppercase and Lowercase/Underscored</u>

five-space indentation for paragraphs

double-spaced body

<u>Paragraph Heading——Underscored/Followed by Period.</u>

bottom margin 1"–1½"

1"

2

ir-	irradiate irrational irreconcilable irrecoverable irredeemable irreformable irrefutable irrefutably irregular irregularity irrelevant irremovable irreplaceable irrepressible irresistible irresponsible irreverence irrevocable
mis-	misapply misbelief miscall misconduct miscue misdirection misfeasance misfire misfit misgiving misguided misinform misjudge mislead mismanage misnomer misplace misprint mispronounce misrepresent misshapen mistake mistaken mistreat mistrial mistrust misunderstand misuse misword
non-	nonabrasive nonaligned nonattached nonbeliever nonchallenging noncolor noncombatant nonconformity noncritical nondenominational nondurable non-Euclidean nonfactual nonfiction nonglare nonjudgmental nonprofit nonresident nonresistant nonreturnable nonstrategic nontaxable non-U nonunion nonverbal nonviolent
over-	overact overage overburden overcompensation overdrive overdue overhead overinflate overnight overpopulate overrun overseas oversee oversimplify oversleep overstock oversupply overtax overthrow overtime overturn overview
per-	perceive perception perfect performance perfume perfunctory perish perjure perjury perpetrate perpetual perpetuate perpetuity perquisite
pre-	preamble prearrange preaxial prebuilt precaution precede preceding precipitate preclude preconceived precook predate predict predispose preempt prefab preflight prehistoric prelaw preliminary premarital premed prepay prevent

Module 11
REPORTS AND MANUSCRIPTS

Written reports are a prime method of obtaining and communicating information. Reports are often written in the third person and deal with facts. A report can take the form of an outline, memorandum, formal report, or graphic illustration.

User Manual
Refer to your User Manual for the following:

- Outlines
- Table of Contents
- Margins
- Page Breaks
- Single and Double Spacing
- Pagination
- Charts and Tables
- Bulleted or Numbered Lists
- Superscripts
- Tabs (with leaders)
- Headers and Footers
- Footnotes and Endnotes or Works Cited
- Indexes

Styling for Formal Reports

Headings
The main heading and chapter headings should be 2" from the top of the page. They are generally centered.

Margins
1. When the report is to be top-bound, use 1" side margins, 1½" top margins, and 1" bottom margins. The first page should have a 2" top margin.
2. When the report is to be left-bound, use 1½" side margins and 1" top margins.
3. When the report is to be unbound (stapled in the upper left corner), use 1" margins all around.

Paragraphs
Paragraphs should be indented 5–7 spaces from the left margin. Some writers do not indent the first paragraph that follows a major heading. This is either company style or individual preference.

pro-	proactive proceed proceedings proclaim produce production profane profess professional profit profound profuse program programmer prologue pronoun pronounce prophetic proportion prorate proscribe proscription prosecution protract
re-	react rebuild recede receive reception recital reclaim re-claim reclamation recollect re-collect recreation re-creation recreational reenter refill refine reform rehabilitate rehearse reimburse relapse relaxation relay release relief relieve remedial reproach reputation repute research residence residuary resigned resume
self-	self-addressed self-assured self-centered self-contained self-control self-educated self-employed self-evident self-governing self-importance self-indulgence self-mailing self-protection self-reliant self-righteous self-rule self-styled self-supporting self-sustaining self-taught self-worth
sub-	subcabinet subcenter subcommittee subdebutante subdirectory subdue subflooring subhuman subject sublease submarine submerge suborbital subordinate subplot subpoena subscript subsoil substantial substitute subtract suburban subway
super-	superficial superfine superfluous supergalaxy superimpose superintendent superior superiority superjet superlative superman supermarket supernatural supernova supersaturate superscript superscription supersede superstore supervise

Brain Buster #11: *Seascapes*

Type the "nautical" expressions used for the following:

Example: tough it out = weather the storm

1. is rigid
2. rescue
3. from first to last
4. have resentment
5. Watch out!
6. maintain the status quo
7. finished
8. make things easy
9. avoid
10. between a rock and a hard place

---

trans-	transact transcontinental transfer transfigure transformer transgression transient transilluminate transistor translate transliterate translucent transmission transmit transoceanic transparent transpire transplant
un-	unbearable unconscious unconstitutional uncontrollable uncountable undo undue unemployed uneventful unfortunate unnecessary
under-	underage underbid undercoat undercurrent undercut underdog underfoot undergo undergraduate underground underline underpaid underpass underrate undersecretary undersell undershirt undersized underskirt understaff underwrite

Suffixes

-able	changeable comfortable laughable mailable preventable remarkable unquestionable unthinkable
-age	bandage bondage breakage brokerage coinage cordage dosage drainage lineage mileage parentage passage portage postage roughage steerage storage tillage tonnage usage verbiage vicarage wreckage
-al	acquittal additional arrival betrayal central classical conventional denial egotistical fatal fiscal general literal logical magical mechanical medical neutral parental proposal rebuttal recital refusal retrieval rival several signal
-ance	absorptance acceptance clearance continuance elegance endurance grievance ignorance importance performance remembrance significance

Your Street Address
City, State ZIP
Current Date

[Person]
[Company]
[Street Address]
[City, State ZIP]

Dear [Person]:

Your advertisement in the BOSTON GLOBE for an
Administrative Assistant is of great interest to
me. As you can see from the enclosed resume, I have
spent the last five years as the Administrative
Assistant to the President of The Rolfe Data Company
and currently supervise two secretaries.

My background includes strong computer skills. I
have worked extensively with Microsoft Word and
WordPerfect 5.2 and have prepared newsletters and
viewgraph presentations. I also have a working
knowledge of Lotus 1-2-3 and basic bookkeeping
skills. My responsibilities have included setting up
trade shows and conferences, as well as making
travel arrangements.

Please give me the opportunity to meet with you
personally to discuss the contribution I can make
to [specific company]. I will call your office
next week to arrange a mutually convenient time.

Sincerely,

Your Name

Enclosure

-ary	auxiliary boundary centenary contrary dictionary elementary evolutionary honorary imaginary infirmary library literary revolutionary secondary secretary stationary tertiary tributary vocabulary voluntary
-ence	absence audience coherence consequence deference dependence emergence existence experience impertinence independence occurrence
-ful, -fuls	careful cupful cupfuls eventful graceful grateful handful harmful helpful meaningful mindful mouthful mouthfuls powerful spoonful spoonfuls tablespoonful teaspoonful thoughtful useful
-fully	carefully gracefully hopefully meaningfully mindfully regretfully thoughtfully willfully
-graph	autograph choreograph chronograph cryptograph epigraph lithograph logograph mimeograph monograph petrograph phonograph pictograph radiograph seismograph telegraph
-graphy	autobiography biography cinematography petrography stenography typography
-ible	accessible admissible deductible eligible feasible incorrigible intelligible invincible possible reversible tangible transmissible
-ing	accommodating accounting bookkeeping carrying conforming copying dining directing forcing hanging marketing painting performing puzzling reforming relaxing sitting standing studying vacating vacuuming worrying worshiping yachting

each person's activities for the week that can be used for each of our departments. He is looking for meaningful statistics (if that isn't a contradiction in terms . . .) that will reflect the contribution each of us is making. ¶ I am proposing that we include the following as part of our weekly status reports:

- Hours of research, planning, and coordination
- Pages drafted
- Pages reviewed and corrected
- Final page count

I would welcome your suggestions and comments regarding the above so that I can put together a final proposal for Harry that reflects an accurate account of how productive we are.

Customized Form Letters

User Manual Customized form letters (also known as Print Merge or Mail Merge) will allow you to prepare form letters and customize them so that each one appears to be an original. Refer to your User Manual for instructions.

EXERCISE 12

Type the form letter that follows and customize it for each of the three recipients:

(1)   Mr. Robert Littlehale, President
      Beth Wolf Employment Services
      205 Minolta Street
      Malden, MA 02148

(2)   Ms. Betty Gau
      The Green Mountain Company
      66 Warburton Circle
      Salem, MA 01970

(3)   Director of Human Resources
      Attleboro Chemical Company, Inc.
      456 Main Street
      Worcester, MA 01602

-ion	appreciation companion consideration correction corrosion description diction exploration explosion fashion habitation invasion irritation notation permission recreation separation
-ish	boyish brownish childish Danish diminish fiendish Finnish girlish greenish limpish Polish prudish reddish selfish Spanish Swedish yellowish
-ism	Americanism atheism Communism conservatism criticism favoritism federalism feminism feudalism fundamentalism hedonism industrialism Judaism mannerism modernism plagiarism skepticism Socialism synergism Zionism
-ist	antagonist atheist chauvinist columnist communist exhibitionist hedonist fatalist fundamentalist industrialist novelist isolationist Methodist pianist protagonist realist segregationist
-ize	agonize burglarize characterize hypnotize itemize localize modernize ostracize revolutionize
-less	careless cordless countless fearless fruitless hapless heartless meaningless meatless mindless motionless odorless passionless profitless speechless spineless spotless thoughtless
-logy	anthology anthropology biology cardiology climatology cosmology ethnology genealogy gerontology gynecology histology kinesiology neurology ontology phonology psychology radiology technology terminology zoology

be interested in planting your roots in the Greater Boston area. In case you are not familiar with the area, I've enclosed an area-wide map together with business information from the Chamber of Commerce. I'm also enclosing a copy of our company's brochure, which lists the buildings we manage. They are all mostly rented at this time, but we predict that there will be vacancies soon because several of our tenants have expressed an interest in larger quarters. We shall try to meet their requirements in our new facility. ¶ In addition to reading our literature, please feel free to call any time or—better yet—pay us a visit. Just call a few days in advance, and we'll be happy to make all the arrangements./Sincerely,/Enclosures

EXERCISE 10

Memorandum

Date/To: Our Staff/From: [your name]/Subject: Magazine Subscriptions/Several months ago I distributed a questionnaire requesting information about the magazines you would like us to order for the office. Based on your responses, we are pleased to inform you that we have subscribed to the following magazines, which I hope will be of value: INC, MODERN OFFICE TECHNOLOGY, and PC MAGAZINE./I would appreciate your comments and future recommendations.

EXERCISE 11

Memorandum

Date/To: Fellow Publications Systems Chiefs/From: Eric L. Lindsell/Re: Reporting for Technical Writing/As you know, Harry Lorenz is in the process of preparing a new method of evaluating

-ly	brotherly casually duly easterly fatherly formally formerly happily merrily motherly northerly only professionally readily quickly respectfully shortly sincerely sisterly southerly steadily truly verily westerly
-ment	acknowledgment adornment advancement advertisement appeasement arrangement assignment defacement encouragement endorsement entanglement estrangement figment judgment management pigment placement procurement supplement
-ous	adventurous analogous dangerous desirous famous ferrous grievous hazardous hideous joyous libelous marvelous mischievous momentous mountainous murderous outrageous perilous poisonous religious ravenous riotous slanderous
-ure	disclosure enclosure erasure foreclosure fracture judicature lecture legislature literature manufacture puncture rupture structure torture

enclosed is a photostatic copy of my check No. 232 in the amount of $422.20, which is proof of payment. ¶ I trust that my insurance will be reinstated and that this matter will be straightened out immediately. Thank you./

EXERCISE 9

Two-Page Letter (Any Style You Choose)

Date/Mr. Harold Roberts/H&R Roberts, Inc./267 Dallas Parkway/Cambridge, MA 02142-1093 /Dear Mr. Roberts:/Debbie Hahn, my associate, suggested that I contact you regarding office space in the Greater Boston area. We are owners and developers of industrial, commercial, and office buildings and would like to be helpful in satisfying your office requirements. ¶ At present we have space available in our Metro Office Complex, which is located between Broadway and Main Street in Cambridge. This affords direct access to Boston and many of the area's academic institutions via the "T" and provides easy access to Logan Airport. We are expecting this building to be ready for occupancy in September of this year. The building will contain some very desirable office suites on the seventh and eighth floors, which have not yet been rented——many with beautiful views of the Charles River. ¶ In Worcester, Massachusetts, which is in the central part of the state, we have just completed the construction of a ten-story office complex that has been described as one of the outstanding office complexes in the Commonwealth of Massachusetts, and we expect the facility in Cambridge to be on a par. ¶ I'm enclosing floor plans of these two buildings. Inasmuch as so much space has already been rented, I encourage you to look at these floor plans as soon as possible if you genuinely think you might

Brain Buster #9:   Who's Afraid

Phobias are abnormal fears. Type the phobia associated with the following fears.

Example: fear of changes = tropophobia

1. closed spaces
2. open spaces
3. water
4. strangers
5. words
6. blood
7. heights
8. darkness
9. marriage
10. getting peanut butter stuck to the roof of your mouth

Semiblock Style

Date/Ms. Arlene Karp, Vice President/Marvin
Industries, Inc./7 Appleland Road/Parsippany, NJ
07054/Dear Ms. Karp:/I thank you for the time you
spent with me at the interview yesterday and
hope that you will give me the chance to put my
resourcefulness and enthusiasm to work for you. ¶
While reading through some of the literature you
gave me, light bulbs started flashing with ideas
for collaterals, one of which is using the icons
from the program to represent features of the
software. ¶ I am excited about the challenges
ahead and look forward to making a major
contribution to the marketing communications
efforts at Marvin Industries./Yours truly,/

Simplified Style

Date/Mal-Ed Corporation/Attn: Becky Gentry,
National Sales Manager/24 Airmont Road/Owasso,
OK 74055/We are interested in installing vending
machines in the lunchroom instead of having the
coffee truck visit our facility. We would like
machines that dispense coffee, soda, juice, and
light snacks. ¶ Our main concern is the limited
amount of space available in our small lunchroom;
therefore, we would like to have one of your
representatives visit us to discuss the
feasibility of such an installation./Sincerely,/

Simplified Style

Date/Ms. Ethel Lorenz/Sharfin Insurance Company/
3 Ternure Avenue/San Francisco, CA 94120-7439/
Re: Policy No. 7216A/In accordance with our
telephone conversation of this afternoon,

Practical Applications

Module 9
CHARTS, TABLES AND COLUMNS

CHARTS AND TABLES

Charts and tables are useful for presenting columns and rows of tabular information. (Columns run vertically and rows run horizontally.) They are also useful for creating invoices, purchase orders, and other forms.

COLUMNS

Columns are useful for information to be presented in a format of two or more columns.

User Manual Refer to your User Manual for the following:

- Tables
- Rows and Columns
- Columnization
- Tabs
- Leaders (also known as Dot Leaders)
- Borders and Boxes

10010/Dear Beth:/I have recently been accepted as part of the master's program at Northeastern University starting with the fall term. This will offer me the opportunity to continue my education, as I have been wanting to do for so long, and be closer to my family. It is with very mixed emotions, therefore, that I am tendering my resignation. ¶ I thoroughly enjoyed being part of your organization for the past five years and greatly value your friendship and all the experiences I've had. My association with you has given me great insight, confidence, and empathy. I hope you will visit me when you are in the Boston area. ¶ Although I am delivering this letter to you personally, I wanted to put in writing how wonderful and memorable these years have been./Fondly,/

EXERCISE 5

Semiblock Style

Date/CERTIFIED MAIL, RETURN RECEIPT REQUESTED/ Joseph Wheeler, Esq./324 Broadway/Somerville, MA 02145/Dear Mr. Wheeler:/Re: Lease Agreement/ Enclosed please find the original and two copies of the lease agreement you sent me on behalf of your clients, Richard and Patricia Schmidt. As per our telephone conversation of this morning, I have deleted Paragraph 12 dealing with payment of utilities, and my initials appear next to the deleted portion. ¶ As soon as Mr. and Mrs. Schmidt have executed their portions of the lease and have returned my copy, I will forward my check in the amount of $1,500./Very truly yours,/enc.

Timed Typings

A table arranges information in tabulated rows and	10
columns. Rows run from left to right while columns	20
run from top to bottom. Tables must be prepared in	30
a format that is uncluttered and easy to read. And	40
a table in a formal report should be enclosed in a	50
border and numbered and titled. Whether your table	60
is formal or informal, be sure the material is ac-	70
curate, precise, and captures the material easily.	80

```
1    2    3    4    5    6    7    8    9    10
```

If you are bound by a style sheet, check that	10
style sheet for items such as how the column heads	20
are to be capitalized, whether they should be bold	30
or italic, whether they should be right aligned or	40
left aligned or centered. You should be consistent	50
in the style and position of captions, titles, and	60
all other information.	64

```
1    2    3    4    5    6    7    8    9    10
```

CHARTS AND TABLES

Type the following exercises as they appear. Remember to align all decimals.

Two Columns

EXERCISE 1

• *decimal lignment in second column*

Invoice Number	Unit Price
344306	$1,000.00
454654	250.00
540567	790.50
458451	550.00
954611	375.50

will continue to employ the high ideals and standards you've set. ¶ Before you leave for Arizona, please give me a call, because I would like to take you out for lunch for old time's sake./Sincerely,/

EXERCISE 3

Modified Block Style

Date/Mr. and Mrs. Gary Sullivan/66 Smith Hill Road/Essex Junction, VT 05452/Dear Mr. and Mrs. Sullivan:/We would you like to take this opportunity to welcome you and your family to Vermont and hope that you will spend many happy years in our area—one of the most beautiful places in the country. We have enclosed one of our calendars, which will introduce you to many of the businesses and recreational facilities in the area. ¶ While you are familiarizing yourselves with the surroundings, please stop by our bank. We extend to our customers the highest allowable interest rates, free checking account facilities, safe deposit boxes, low interest loans, direct payment of utility bills, and the personalized service of our staff. For your convenience, we are open Mondays through Fridays from 9 AM to 3:30 PM, on Friday evenings from 7 PM to 9 PM, and on Saturday mornings from 9 AM to noon. ¶ The enclosed $25 gift certificate can be used to open your first savings account with us./ Sincerely,/Enclosure

EXERCISE 4

Modified Block Style

Date/PERSONAL/Elisabeth Wolf/Wolf Jewelry Exchange/305 Fifth Avenue/Suite 100/New York, NY

```
┌─────────────────────────────────────────────────────────────┐
│              HOLIDAYS AND CELEBRATIONS                       │
│                                                             │
│   Holiday                  Date                             │
│                                                             │
│   New Year's Day           January 1                       │
│   Lincoln's Birthday       February 12                     │
│   Washington's Birthday    February 22                     │
│   St. Patrick's Day        March 17                        │
│   Memorial Day             Last Monday in May              │
│   Independence Day         July 4                          │
│   Labor Day                First Monday in September       │
│   Columbus Day             October 12                      │
│   Veteran's Day            November 11                     │
│   Thanksgiving             Fourth Thursday in November     │
│   Christmas                December 25                     │
│                                                             │
└─────────────────────────────────────────────────────────────┘
```

Three Columns

EXERCISE 3

Employee	Social Security Number	Hourly Rate
James Smith	122-45-2454	$10.00
Elizabeth Doe	245-35-5678	5.90
Susan Britton	136-35-7863	7.50
John Green	245-56-3557	11.20
Grace Jones	574-46-5675	6.75
Barbara Adams	075-36-7753	8.75
Zelda Nasip	135-43-6753	8.50

Type the following letters using the letter style indicated and prepare an envelope for each. Be certain that placement is correct and that each letter is centered both vertically and horizontally. Use the current date and sign your name to each letter. The slash (/) indicates the start of a new line, and the paragraph marker (¶) indicates the start of a new paragraph.

EXERCISE 1

Full Block Style

Date/Marc Alan & Associates/24 Besen Parkway/Box 5100/New York, New York 10150-5100/Dear Mr. Alan:/Please consider me for the entry-level architect position you are advertising in the Sunday edition of THE NEW YORK TIMES. ¶ As you can see from the enclosed resume, I recently graduated from Massachusetts Institute of Technology with a 3.8 average and spent two years working part-time as a draftsman. I spent summers during high school working as an electrician getting hands-on experience in the building field. Also, I am well versed in CAD/CAM and many other computer applications. While attending college, I was president of Sigma Chi fraternity and was an active member of the debating team and computer club. ¶ Please give me the opportunity to discuss my background at a personal interview. You can reach me at (212) 745-1235./Very truly yours,/Enclosure

EXERCISE 2

Full Block Style

Date/Mr. Marvin Karp/7 Appleland Road/Chicago, IL 60602/Dear Marv:/It is with great pleasure that I read of your much deserved promotion to Sales Manager of the Southwest region. This honor couldn't have been bestowed upon a more enthusiastic, hard-working, and deserving person. ¶ All of us here in Chicago will miss you but

EXERCISE 4

```
┌──────────────────────────────────────────────────────────┐
│                    PUBLISHING LIST                       │
│                                                          │
│   TITLE                     AUTHOR          DATE         │
│   Data Processing           Michula         1989         │
│   Public Speaking           Wolverin        1990         │
│   Let's Talk Business       Smitherson      1992         │
│   Business English          Reed            1991         │
│                                                          │
└──────────────────────────────────────────────────────────┘
```

EXERCISE 5

```
┌──────────────────────────────────────────────────────────┐
│                   SIGNS OF THE ZODIAC                    │
│                                                          │
│   SIGN              COMMON NAME       DATES              │
│   Aries             Ram                3/21 - 4/19       │
│   Taurus            Bull               4/10 - 5/20       │
│   Gemini            Twins              5/21 - 6/20       │
│   Cancer            Crab               6/21 - 7/22       │
│   Leo               Lion               7/23 - 8/22       │
│   Virgo             Virgin             8/23 - 9/22       │
│   Libra             Balance            9/23 - 10/22      │
│   Scorpio           Scorpion          10/23 - 11/21      │
│   Sagittarius       Archer            11/22 - 12/21      │
│   Capricorn         Goat              12/22 - 1/19       │
│   Aquarius          Water-bearer       1/20 - 2/18       │
│   Pisces            Fish               2/19 - 3/20       │
│                                                          │
└──────────────────────────────────────────────────────────┘
```

Folding and Inserting a Letter

For a Large Envelope

1. Fold the bottom face up, slightly less than one third of the length, and make a crease.

2. Fold the top third down and make a crease. This will enable the reader to view the letterhead before reading the contents of the letter.

3. Insert the letter with the last crease directed toward the bottom of the envelope.

For a Small Envelope

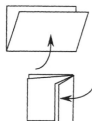

1. Fold the bottom face up, slightly less than a half inch from the top.

2. Fold the right side one third to the left.

3. Fold the remaining third to the right and make a crease.

4. Insert the letter with the last crease directed toward the bottom of the envelope.

Four Columns

EXERCISE 6

TWO-LETTER STATE ABBREVIATIONS

Alabama	AL	Missouri	MO
Alaska	AK	Montana	MT
Arizona	AZ	Nebraska	NE
Arkansas	AR	Nevada	NV
California	CA	New Hampshire	NH
Canal Zone	CZ	New Jersey	NJ
Colorado	CO	New Mexico	NM
Connecticut	CT	New York	NY
Delaware	DE	North Carolina	NC
District of		North Dakota	ND
Columbia	DC	Ohio	OH
Florida	FL	Oklahoma	OK
Georgia	GA	Oregon	OR
Guam	GU	Pennsylvania	PA
Hawaii	HI	Puerto Rico	PR
Idaho	ID	Rhode Island	RI
Illinois	IL	South Carolina	SC
Indiana	IN	South Dakota	SD
Iowa	IA	Tennessee	TN
Kansas	KS	Texas	TX
Kentucky	KY	Utah	UT
Louisiana	LA	Vermont	VT
Maine	ME	Virginia	VA
Maryland	MD	Virgin Islands	VI
Massachusetts	MA	Washington	WA
Michigan	MI	West Virginia	WV
Minnesota	MN	Wisconsin	WI
Mississippi	MS	Wyoming	WY

Preparing the Envelope

The post office is using optical character readers (OCRs) in many large cities to expedite mail processing and delivery and is requesting adherence to the following guidelines in order to increase the speed and accuracy of mail delivery:

- Type the address in all capital letters and don't use punctuation marks.
- If there isn't a preprinted return address, type your name and return address in the upper left corner.
- If there is an attention line in your mailing address, place it on the first line, above the company name.
- Use capitalized abbreviations for directions (N, E, NE), streets (ST, AVE, RD, BLVD), suites or units (STE, APT, RM), etc.
- Type the ZIP code on the last line of the address, two spaces or three spaces to the right of the two-letter state abbreviation.

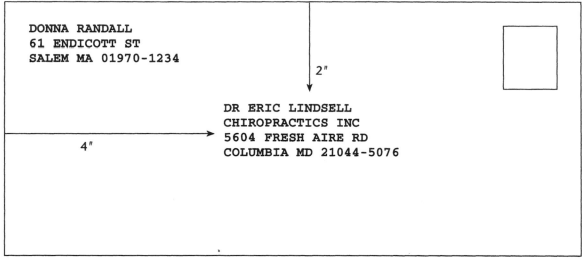

LARGE (NO. 10) ENVELOPE

EXERCISE 7

• *right justify second column and use leaders*

```
                    MILESTONES
Approval of concepts . . . . . . . . . . . I
Availability of resources . . . . . . . . II
Effective operating procedures for
    evaluating benefits . . . . . . . . .III
Postdeployment ABC operational
    assessment by manager . . . . . . . . IV
Planning for existing assessment . . . . . V
```

EXERCISE 8

The following is a list of commonly misspelled cities. Supply the appropriate state abbreviation. (The answers appear at the end of this module.)

```
                COMMONLY MISSPELLED CITIES
Akron              OH        Memphis            TN
Albuquerque                  Miami
Baton Rouge                  Milwaukee
Beaumont                     Minneapolis
Berkeley                     New Orleans
Bridgeport                   Omaha
Buffalo                      Philadelphia
Chattanooga                  Phoenix
Chicago                      Pittsburgh
Cincinnati                   Racine
Cleveland                    Raleigh
Des Moines                   San Francisco
Detroit                      Savannah
Duluth                       Seattle
Gary                         Shreveport
Honolulu                     Syracuse
Knoxville                    Tucson
Lincoln                      Wilkes-Barre
Louisville                   Wilmington
Macon                        Worcester
```

Memorandum Type this memorandum as it appears. Supply the current date and type your initials instead of *xx*. A memo does not have to be vertically centered and the heading may vary.

```
Date:      Current

To:        All Office Personnel

From:      Melissa G. Lavrusky

Subject:   Proper Memo Style


The main purpose of a memo is to transmit
ideas, decisions, suggestions, etc., to other
members of an organization. If the organization
uses memos frequently, it will generally have
printed memo forms.

The heading should contain the four elements
you see above, but the placement can vary
slightly.

On a memo the inside address, salutation, and
complimentary closing are eliminated. The body
starts three lines below the heading.

xx
```

EXERCISE 9

• *right justify*
Arabic numerals
• *left justify*
Roman
numerals

ROMAN NUMERALS

1	I		30	XXX
2	II		35	XXV
3	III		40	XL
4	IV		50	L
5	V		60	LX
6	VI		70	LXX
7	VII		80	LXXX
8	VIII		90	XC
9	IX		100	C
10	X		200	CC
11	XI		300	CCC
12	XII		400	CD
13	XIII		500	D
14	XIV		600	DC
15	XV		700	DCC
16	XVI		800	DCCC
17	XVII		900	CM
18	XVIII		1000	M
19	XIX		1500	MD
20	XX		1800	MDCCC
21	XXI		1890	MDCCCXC
22	XXII		1920	MCMXX
23	XXIII		1950	MCML
24	XXIV		1959	MCMLIX
25	XXV		2000	MM

Mr. and Mrs. Harold Roberts
Page 2
Date

5. The second page of a two-page letter should
be on plain bond paper, not letterhead.
Start the page with the name of the addressee,
a Page 2 notation, and the date.

6. The second page of the letter should not be
vertically centered. It should include at least
two lines of text.

I have enclosed a pamphlet on letter writing
that you should find useful. If I can be of
further help, don't hesitate to contact me.

Sincerely,

Jon A. Roberts

xx
Enclosure

EXERCISE 10

Type the full text of this two-page report.

Business Successes

- Has value on an individual basis and on a component basis during the cycle.
- Speeds up the user requirements analysis and yields better results than traditional approaches.
- Involves compressing the normal interviewing sessions into intensive group participation workshops.

Advantages

- Results are comprehensive because all the concerned people are involved.
- It achieves buy-off for a given project because everyone is made aware of the information needed.
- The group comes to a consensus regarding the necessary functionality and to the priorities of these functions. This is especially helpful in the qualifying and scoping process.

Participants

- Workshop leader.
- Users of the proposed system.
- Business personnel familiar with the current processes.
- Technical personnel familiar with the existing or proposed new systems.
- Scribe.

Type this two-page full block letter as it appears. Supply the current date and type your initials instead of *xx*. Be certain that placement of the parts of the letter is correct and that the letter is vertically and horizontally centered on the first page and horizontally centered on the second page.

Date

Mr. and Mrs. Harold Roberts
213 Hollywood Avenue
Dallas, TX 75208

Dear Harold and Lorraine:

In response to your letter of October 12, the following are answers to the questions you posed:

1. The salutation "Dear Sir:" is no longer appropriate when you don't know if the reader is a man or a woman. I would recommend that you use "Dear Sir or Madam:" instead.

2. The subject line is considered part of the letter, not part of the heading. Therefore, it should always be placed two spaces below the salutation. The purpose of the subject line is to direct the reader's attention to the theme of the letter.

3. If additional material will accompany the letter, an enclosure notation should appear at the bottom. This calls the reader's attention to the fact that something besides the letter should be in the envelope.

4. When a copy of the letter is being sent to a third party, a *cc* (carbon copy) notation is typed directly below the enclosure notation. Today, very few, if any, companies are using actual carbon copies, so the letters *pc* (for "photostatic copy") are starting to appear in place of *cc*.

KEY PEOPLE	ROLE/SKILLS NEEDED
Leader	• run the meetings. • keep the group on track. • have excellent communication skills. • feel very comfortable working in front of a group.
Scribe	• record the proceedings of the meetings. • take care to divide the proceedings into the following categories: data models, information usages, perceived problem areas, solutions and incentives, unresolved (open) issues, unanswered questions.

COLUMNS

First, type "So You Want to Be a Writer!" as a single-column report, using left justification. Second, convert the report you typed into two columns. Third, convert the report into three columns. See an example of the two- and three-column conversion following the single-column format.

Note

If you are using a font other than Courier 12, your report will not match this one on a line-by-line basis.

Simplified Style Type this simplified letter as it appears. Supply the current date and type your initials instead of *xx*. Be certain that placement of the parts of the letter is correct and that the letter is vertically and horizontally centered.

```
Date


Ms. Nicole Robin
36 Setter Way
Minneapolis, MN 55042


SIMPLIFIED STYLE


You no longer have to be concerned with
selecting the appropriate salutation or
complimentary closing. This streamlined letter
style is recommended by the Administrative
Management Society and has completely done away
with those troublesome letter openings and
closings.

The subject line (with no notation) appears in
capital letters three lines below the inside
address, and the body appears three lines below
the subject line. The writer's name is typed
four lines below the body and is also in
capital letters. Note that everything is flush
with the left margin.

Although this letter style is not commonly
used, it is expected to become more popular in
the future because it is less time-consuming to
prepare, thereby less costly.



JON A. ROBERTS

xx
```

SO YOU WANT TO BE A WRITER!

Everyone has a story to tell or valuable information they'd like to share. Some manuscripts get published and others merely collect dust on the author's bookshelf. Not everyone becomes a household legend like Agatha Christie or James Michener, let alone William Shakespeare, but there is hope for us—for the unknowns. After all, every famous author was once an unknown.

If you want to write a book and are serious about getting it published, you must be armed with a computer, a current edition of the WRITER'S MARKET (updated annually), and thick skin. I include *thick skin* because the stream of rejections can be devastating. One thing you must remember: A publisher is never rejecting you personally. Writing is subjective, so what may not appeal to one editor in a company may appeal to another. Also, many publishers prepare a five-year publishing plan, and your manuscript might not fit into that plan. (That's a typical rejection excuse.)

MY HUMBLE BEGINNINGS
I never aspired to be a writer; my writing career was spawned quite by accident. I was teaching paralegal skills for a small postsecondary business school. One day, the secretary left me a note saying that a woman from a major dictionary publisher had called and was looking for someone to rewrite a dictionary. Since I'd never worked on dictionaries, I folded the note and (for some unknown reason) tossed it in my pocketbook. Several weeks later the note fell on the floor,

---

Type this semiblock letter as it appears. Supply the current date and type your initials instead of *xx*. Be certain that placement of the parts of the letter is correct and that the letter is vertically and horizontally centered.

```
                                        Date


        Ms. Jacqueline Kim
        36 Lincoln Road
        Monroe, NY 10950

        Dear Ms. Kim:

            Re: Semiblock Style

            The distinguishing features of this letter
        style are that the subject line is indented
        below the salutation and all paragraphs are
        indented five to seven spaces from the left
        margin.

            It is important to remember that two tabs
        must be used: one for the date and the compli-
        mentary closing and one for the indentation
        of the subject line and paragraphs.

            If you are in a situation where maximum
        productivity is not essential, this may be your
        preferred style.

                                    Sincerely,


                                    Jon A. Roberts


        xx
```

and I thought, "Um, perhaps this is an omen. Let me call this woman Colleen and see what it's all about." (I had always gotten A's on my "What I Did On My Summer Vacation" reports. And I had just been to a Chinese restaurant, and my fortune cookie read, "You will soon change your line of work.") To make a long story short, I got the assignment to write a major chapter for a legal secretarial handbook.

Thereafter, I just knew that the world was waiting for my pearly words! So I put together the beginnings of a manuscript for a book about women returning to the job market. This was back in the 1960's when the idea was relatively new and women were looking for direction and encouragement. I checked what was then the current edition of WRITER'S MARKET (more about that later) and located all the publishers in that genre. I simultaneously submitted the manuscript to several publishers and had nightly dreams of the bidding wars in which they would all be vying to win me over. Well, was I in for a rude awakening. I was rejected by an honor roll of prestigious as well as unknown publishers and could have wallpapered the entire Taj Mahal with their letters. As a matter of fact, I had gotten so used to rejections, I was expecting one from my mother. What kept me going was—I remembered that Margaret Mitchell's timeless novel, GONE WITH THE WIND, was rejected endlessly along with a host of other well-known classics.

I had spent what was equivalent to the national debt on postage but didn't give up. Finally, two long, grueling years later, I got a positive response from one publisher. It was not the response I had expected, but it was positive nonetheless. An editor from a New York publishing

Type this modified block letter as it appears. Supply the current date and type your initials instead of *xx*. Be certain that placement of the parts of the letter is correct and that the letter is vertically and horizontally centered.

```
                                        Date


        Mr. Eric Laurence
        23 Northeastern Avenue
        Columbia, MD 21044

        Dear Mr. Laurence:

        Re: Modified Block Style

        Modified block has traditionally been the most
        commonly used of all letter styles.

        The most noted difference between this style
        and the full block style is that the date and
        complimentary closing are slightly to the right
        of center. Note that the subject line, the
        inside address, and all paragraphs remain flush
        with the left margin.

        This letter style is very appealing to the eye
        and is very popular.


                                    Sincerely,



                                    Jon A. Roberts

        xx
```

house had read my manuscript and liked my style of writing. Although that publisher didn't publish the manuscript, I was offered a contract for a book that was compatible with my background. That book has just gone into its third edition, and I have had others published. My determination did pay off.

By the way, my original manuscript of women returning to the job market is still collecting dust on my bookshelf. By now the subject matter is passé and the pages are yellow.

GETTING STARTED

I caution against writing a book in its entirety unless you have a publisher. If you don't find a publisher, you've expended a lot of effort. Instead, write a complete chapter and prepare a fully annotated outline. In most cases, that's all a publisher will require for review purposes. (The manuscript should be double-spaced, single-sided, with 1" margins all around.)

The WRITER'S MARKET—an author's bible—will give you all the information you need to submit your manuscript: how to write a query letter, the editor in chief of each publishing house, each publisher's specialty, royalty arrangements, and much more. Always include a self-addressed stamped envelope so your manuscript can be returned. (And don't worry about copyrighting your work. No reputable publisher will print your material without your permission.) Then you wear out the soles of your shoes trekking to the mailbox each day waiting for responses. And then, after your frustration level has tipped the Richter scale and you've given up all hope of seeing your name in print, you get that one, wonderful *yes*.

Letters and Memorandum Styles

Full Block Style Type this full block letter as it appears. Supply the current date and type your initials instead of *xx*. Be certain that placement of the parts of the letter is correct and that the letter is vertically and horizontally centered.

```
Date


Mr. Marc Alan
345 Peachtree Place, NW
Atlanta, GA 30318

Dear Mr. Alan:

Re: Full Block Style

This easy-to-keyboard letter style is becoming
more and more popular and is widely used in
many of today's modern offices.

It is a very efficient style because everything
begins at the left margin, thereby eliminating
the need to set tabs or be concerned about
whether the date and complimentary closing are
too far to the left or right. We are now in an
era where productivity is a major concern;
therefore, this letter style will, over a
period of time, increase the flow of paperwork.

I hope you will consider using this new style
as you prepare for the office you will soon be
opening.

Very truly yours,


Jon A. Roberts

xx
```

Two-Column Format

SO YOU WANT TO BE A WRITER!

Everyone has a story to tell or valuable information they'd like to share. Some manuscripts get published and others merely collect dust on the author's bookshelf. Not everyone becomes a household legend like Agatha Christie or James Michener, let alone William Shakespeare, but there is hope for us—for the unknowns. After all, every famous author was once an unknown.

If you want to write a book and are serious about getting it published, you must be armed with a computer, a current edition of the WRITER'S MARKET (updated annually), and thick skin. I include *thick skin* because the stream of rejections can be devastating. One thing you must remember: A publisher is never rejecting you personally. Writing is subjective, so what may not appeal to one editor in a company may appeal to another. Also, many publishers prepare a five-year publishing plan, and your manuscript might not fit into that plan. (That's a typical rejection excuse.)

Three-Column Format

SO YOU WANT TO BE A WRITER!

Everyone has a story to tell or valuable information they'd like to share. Some manuscripts get published and others merely collect dust on the author's bookshelf. Not everyone becomes a household legend like Agatha Christie or James Michener, let alone William Shakespeare, but there is hope for us—for the unknowns. After all, every famous author was once an unknown.

If you want to write a book and are serious about getting it published, you must be armed with a computer, a current edition of the WRITER'S MARKET (updated annually), and thick skin. I include *thick skin* because the stream of rejections can be devastating. One thing you must remember: A publisher is never rejecting you personally. Writing is subjective, so what may not appeal to one editor in a company may appeal to another. Also, many publishers prepare a five-year publishing plan,

Dear Fred: 2

    Please be advised that the audition scheduled   12
for Monday, December 13, has been changed. The new   22
date will be Wednesday, December 15. We will still   32
meet at 9:30 A.M. We will break for lunch at about   42
noon and will resume at one. We will also take two   52
15-minute breaks. One in the morning and the other   62
in the afternoon. If the new date should cause you   72
any problems, kindly advise me as soon as you can.   82

1   2   3   4   5   6   7   8   9   10

Dear Mr. Myers: 3

    By now you must have heard the good news! Our   13
division has been selected as the year's recipient   23
of the Kirland International Award for Excellence.   33
It is a great honor and I personally want to thank   43
each one on the team who helped make this division   53
a success. It is people like you whom we are proud   63
to call the company's most treasured assets.   71

1   2   3   4   5   6   7   8   9   10

COMMONLY MISSPELLED CITIES

Akron	OH	Memphis	TN
Albuquerque	NM	Miami	FL
Baton Rouge	LA	Milwaukee	WI
Beaumont	TX	Minneapolis	MN
Berkeley	CA	New Orleans	LA
Bridgeport	CT	Omaha	NE
Buffalo	NY	Philadelphia	PA
Chattanooga	TN	Phoenix	AZ
Chicago	IL	Pittsburgh	PA
Cincinnati	OH	Racine	WI
Cleveland	OH	Raleigh	NC
Des Moines	IA	San Francisco	CA
Detroit	MI	Savannah	GA
Duluth	MN	Seattle	WA
Gary	IN	Shreveport	LA
Honolulu	HI	Syracuse	NY
Knoxville	TN	Tucson	AZ
Lincoln	NE	Wilkes-Barre	PA
Louisville	KY	Wilmington	DE
Macon	GA	Worcester	MA

Date Line	April 8, 19XX
Mailing or In-House Notation	CERTIFIED MAIL
Inside Address	Marric Production Company
Attention Line	Attention Marc N. Eric
	3 Ternure Avenue
	Monsey, NY 10952
Salutation	Gentlemen:
Subject Line	Re: Letter of Recommendation for Kathy Wertalik

Body (Message)

It is a pleasure to write this letter of recommendation on behalf of Kathy Wertalik. She was in my employ as a part-time secretary/receptionist for five years and left to seek full-time employment with another company. Unfortunately, our company is quite small, and there were no advancement possibilities for her within our organization.

I found Ms. Wertalik to be a person of high integrity, who worked tirelessly and with the highest degree of efficiency. Her tact is unquestionable and her skills are topnotch.

She was a most valued employee, and any company would be most fortunate to have her join its staff.

Complimentary Closing — Sincerely,

Signature Line — Jon A. Roberts

Reference Initials — pt

Enclosure Notation — Enclosure

Copy Notation — cc: Kathy Wertalik

Postscript — I have enclosed a copy of the records you requested.

Brain Buster #10:   Red, White, and Blue

Type the "color" expressions used for the following.

Example: livid = saw red

1. bribery
2. gabs a lot
3. cowardly
4. VIP handling
5. give the go-ahead
6. delighted
7. famous
8. take one's lunch
9. disguise
10. having an unduly optimistic outlook

Signature Line   Horizontal placement of the signature line depends on the letter style selected. Some variations are:

Very truly yours,   Very truly yours,

ROBERTS CONSULTING CO.

                                         John A. Roberts

Jon A. Roberts

Reference Initials   Reference initials are used when someone other than the writer types the letter. Initials always appear at the left margin and include either the writer's and typist's initials or the typist's initials only.

SLR
slr
SRL/JAR

Enclosure Notation   The enclosure notation appears on the line below the reference initials when additional material is included with the letter. The word *Enclosure* is sufficient; however, some people list the enclosures or indicate the number of enclosures. Another option is to use the word *Attachment* for such material.

Enclosure
enc.
Enc. 2 (for number of enclosures)
Attachment

Copy Notation   When a copy of the letter is being sent to a third party, a *cc* notation (held over from the days of carbon copies) is often included. It appears directly below the enclosure notation or reference initials and is followed by the name of the person to whom the copy is being sent. If a photostatic copy is sent, the initials *pc* can be substituted.

   In the event the writer does not want to notify the addressee that a third party will be receiving a copy, a *bc* (blind copy) or *bcc* (blind carbon copy) notation is made on the copy only.

Postscript   A postscript notation is used for emphasis. A postscript should be used sparingly because it could be interpreted as an afterthought, indicating a lack of organization on the part of the writer. A postscript is placed two lines below the last notation without the P.S. notation.

Letters and memos are the second most common form of business communications. The most common is forms.

When you are typing a letter, be concerned with the letter's organization, completeness, accuracy, clarity, and neatness. Also, center the letter vertically and horizontally, forming an imaginary frame around the text. When you finish the letter, you should be proud to place your signature or reference initials on it.

Margin Guidelines

Short Letter (approximately 125 words or less)

1½" left and right margins
3" top and bottom margins

Average Letter (approximately 126–225 words)

1¼" left and right margins
2½" top and bottom margins

Long Letter (approximately 226 words or more)

¾"–1" left and right margins
2" top and bottom margins

User Manual

Refer to your User Manual for the following:

- Margins
- Customized Form Letters

Parts of a Business Letter

The following explains all the parts of a letter. Please see the example that follows for a visual display.

Date

Always write the date in full; do not abbreviate.

Mailing or In-House Notation

Mailing notations can be Special Delivery, Certified Mail, or Registered Mail and in-house notations can be Confidential, Please Hold, etc. Each is placed two lines below the date, always at the left margin. They can be capitalized and/or underscored.

Inside Address	The inside address starts four lines below the date (or two lines below the mailing or in-house notation) and includes the name of the person to whom you are writing, the name of the company, the full street address, and the city, state, and ZIP code.
Attention Line	The attention line, which is part of the inside address, is used when you are writing to a company and want the letter directed to a particular person or department. It is presented in one of the following ways:

```
ReMARCable Drafting & Design
561 Banks Street
San Francisco, CA 94110
Attention Marc A. Lindsell

ReMARCable Drafting & Design
Attention Marc A. Lindsell
561 Banks Street
San Francisco, CA 94110
```

Salutation	The salutation is placed two lines below the last line of the address and should correspond to the first line of the inside address.

```
ABC Company . . . . . . . . Ladies or Gentlemen:
Ms. Janice Teisch . . . . . . . Dear Ms. Teisch:
Personnel Director  . . . . . Dear Sir or Madam:
```

Subject or Reference Line	The subject line is considered part of the letter; therefore, it should always be placed two lines below the salutation. Its purpose is to direct the reader to the theme of the letter. Horizontal placement depends on the letter style selected.
Body (Message)	The body of the letter is generally single-spaced with double-spacing between the paragraphs.

- The opening paragraph is generally short. It serves as an introduction.
- The middle paragraph(s) supports the opening. It provides additional information.
- The final paragraph is generally short. It serves as a summation, request, suggestion, or look to the future.

Complimentary Closing	The complimentary closing appears two lines below the last typewritten paragraph line. Horizontal placement depends on the letter style selected.

Letters, Envelopes, and Memos